S0-GQF-472

Arthur Miller's Global Theater

Arthur Miller's Global Theater

Edited by Enoch Brater

The University of Michigan Press

Ann Arbor

WITHDRAWN

OHIO UNIVERSITY LIBRARY ATHENS OHIO

Copyright © by the University of Michigan 2007
All rights reserved
Published in the United States of America by
The University of Michigan Press
Manufactured in the United States of America
⊗ Printed on acid-free paper

2010 2009 2008 2007   4   3   2   1

No part of this publication may be reproduced, stored in a retrieval
system, or transmitted in any form or by any means, electronic,
mechanical, or otherwise, without the written permission of the
publisher.

A CIP catalog record for this book is available from the British Library.

Library of Congress Cataloging-in-Publication Data

Arthur Miller's global theater / edited by Enoch Brater.
    p.   cm.
  ISBN-13: 978-0-472-11593-8 (alk. paper)
  ISBN-10: 0-472-11593-6 (alk. paper)
    1. Miller, Arthur, 1915-2005–Stage history–Foreign countries.
  2. Miller, Arthur, 1915-2005–Appreciation–Foreign countries.
  3. Miller, Arthur, 1915-2005–Adaptations–History and
criticism.   4. Miller, Arthur, 1915-2005–Influence.   I. Brater,
Enoch.

PS3525.I5156Z535   2007
812'.52–dc22   2006102227

For theater friends and colleagues, here and abroad

Acknowledgments

The publication of this volume has been purposefully timed to coincide with the opening of the Arthur Miller Theatre at the new Walgreen Drama Center at the University of Michigan on March 29, 2007. The origin of the project, however, goes back to an earlier moment in the history of Arthur Miller's relationship with his alma mater. In October 2000, as part of the major international symposium held in Ann Arbor to mark the playwright's eighty-fifth birthday, the inaugural session was devoted to a consideration of Miller's drama in a global perspective. That first roundtable proved so successful, incorporating as it did perspectives based on the production history of Miller's plays in Argentina, Japan, England, Israel, Denmark, and Canada, that it made all of us who were present think in wider terms about what happens to a major American writer when his work crosses national borders. *Arthur Miller's Global Theater,* a book that vastly expands the range and implications of our initial discussion, is an attempt to explore this issue more fully and in much wider cultural contexts.

Several colleagues at the University of Michigan have been instrumental in helping me bring this project to fruition: Terrence J. McDonald, the Dean of the College of Literature, Science and the Arts, who has generously supported my writing and research; Lee Doyle, who, as Chief of Staff for former Vice President for Communications Lisa Rudgers, has been a driving force behind this book in its relationship to both the local community and the national presence of the University of Michigan as a whole; and Christopher Kendall, who, early on in his role as Dean of the School of Music, Theatre and Dance, recognized the potential of this volume as a centerpiece for the symposium on "Global Miller" designed to celebrate the opening of the Arthur Miller Theatre. The continuing support from the legendary LeAnn Fields at the University of Michigan Press on this and on so many other projects over the past two decades is something that continues to amaze and inspire me. It should be abundantly clear, too, that the completion of this book could not have taken place without the encouragement of my colleagues in the international theater community. It is, in the final analysis, their vision and their hard work that continues to give Arthur Miller his voice on the world stage.

Contents

RETROSPECTIVES

INTRODUCTION

Enoch Brater

Cross-Cultural Encounters
Arthur Miller and the International Theater Community

When Arthur Miller died at his Connecticut home on February 10, 2005, surrounded by close members of his family, the report of his passing was treated in the national media as a major event. America's most enduring playwright was eighty-nine years old. No one could remember when an obituary of a leading cultural figure had appeared above the fold on the front page of the *New York Times* before. This certainly was not the case for Susan Sontag, who predeceased him by several weeks, or even for Saul Bellow, the Nobel Prize–winning novelist who died, the same age as Miller, only two months later. A similar sense of urgency was also apparent when the public memorial held in his honor took place at the Majestic Theatre in New York the following May. The long line for admission crept down West 44th Street, swung around Schubert Alley, and continued onto West 45th Street. More than fifteen hundred people attended the service, but not everyone was able to get in.

Miller was, of course, the quintessential New Yorker, both by outlook and accent, so it should come as no surprise that his local community would want to pay tribute to its native son in such a conspicuous and meaningful way. And yet it was not only Manhattan that recognized, as Linda Loman does in *Death of a Salesman,* that "attention, attention must finally be paid to such a man." All over the country Miller was celebrated as the last of the twentieth century's theatrical giants, the playwright who, along with Tennessee Williams and Eugene O'Neill, had given a new voice to a modern drama that was distinctly—and tragically—American.

That steadfast Americanism, especially as discussed by fellow play-wrights Edward Albee and Tony Kushner and longtime friends like the Rev. William Sloan Coffin, Jr., and former presidential candidate George McGovern (all of whom spoke at Miller's New York memorial), seems to loom even larger today than it did during his own lifetime. So much so that a close look at the more than fifty-six plays Miller completed now reveals a landscape as vast as Whitman's, a moral center as lucid as Emerson's, and a lyricism as surprisingly eloquent as anything one might find in Hart Crane's epic poem about that mythic gateway known as Brooklyn Bridge. All of this from a writer who liked to say, as he did of *All My Sons,* that what he really wanted to do all along was compose a story "so that you could tell it to a man seated next to you on a train, and he would understand it."[1]

Written "from the sidewalk, not the skyscraper," the "brutally realistic" work Miller wrote about war profiteering defined the big subject that would make him famous: the conflict between public and private morality. *All My Sons,* a drama about "business vs. civilization,"[2] was not so much a play about what was wrong with America as it was about what still needed to be set right in its functioning democracy. He placed his audience in the hot seat. "It's not your guilt I want," he has his character Leduc say to the count in *Incident at Vichy,* a much later play, "it's your responsibility." In 1947, when Elia Kazan's production of *All My Sons* opened on Broadway, the nation, having defeated the Nazis in Europe and Japanese imperialism in the Pacific, was feeling pretty good about itself. At a high point of such triumphalism, the playwright dared to ask questions no one wanted to think about at that or any other time: Who made money out of the death of whose sons? And who stood by and watched it happen? In this play, as so often in Miller, "the chickens come home to roost": Joe Keller, the manufacturer who sold defective airplane parts to the military, must pay the ultimate price for reneging on his part of the social contract. But before he leaves this stage he must be made to realize what his surviving son already knows: all those young pilots who flew off on missions from which they never returned were "all my sons." His final statement, straightforward though it is, nonetheless certifies the power and eloquence Miller extracts from a deceptively simple recognition scene: "And I guess they were, I guess they were." Moments later a shot is heard offstage.

Miller had been trying to write a play like this for some time, one that could be both specific and emblematic at the same time. The workmanlike scripts he wrote in the 1930s while still a student at the University of Michigan, prizewinning efforts like *No Villain* and *They Too Arise,* clearly display a fiery social conscience in search of an adequate dramatic form. But it would take a national crisis like a world war and the consequences of how success was measured in its aftermath to give him the creative push that had eluded him ever since his undergraduate days in Ann Arbor: the maturity to imagine "a totally articulated work instead of an anecdote."

Death of a Salesman, the landmark play that appeared two years later, was, if anything, even more effective in convincing national audiences that there was something fundamentally suspect about a society that venerates material success and then tries to sell it as happiness. "Chasing everything that rusts," Willy Loman, little and local and desperately trying all the time "to write his name on ice on a hot July day," is cast in the unenviable role of Miller's representative man. *He never knew,* however, *who he was.* Willy did indeed have "all the wrong dreams," as we hear Biff intone when it is all too late, but they were nonetheless the same ones nourished as part of some vast cultural reverie. "Be well liked," he tells his sons, "and you shall never want." Go for the gold. Bring home the prize. If you don't "make it," it's your own fault. Create an impression. Don't whistle in elevators. Look the man in the eye. Don't say "gee," a boy's word, not a man's. Win, win, win—and be sure to win big. And this above all: whatever you do, don't get caught. You might as well forget about "to thine own self be true."

So much has been said about *Salesman* as the ultimate postwar critique of the American dream that we may run the risk of underestimating the overwhelming integrity of its emotional power in performance. The playwright initially did so himself. For a long time he thought that what he had really built into his compelling story about Willy Loman's downward trajectory was a sober and objective analysis of a corrupt value system gone horribly awry. But the first audiences for this play in Philadelphia and New York reacted quite differently when they left the theater in tears. Fifty years later Miller came to the reluctant conclusion that, at least in this drama, "I suppose you can't make people see unless they feel."[3]

Death of a Salesman, like *All My Sons* before it, is a work of huge ambition: it aims at nothing less than making theater part of the national conversation. This is "big statement drama" in the tradition of O'Neill, though in Miller's case he was thinking, as usual, about Ibsen ("I might have looked to O'Neill," Miller said, "but I didn't"). He turned to Ibsen again as a model for his initial response to the first wave of Communist witch hunts sweeping the country in the early 1950s, when he adapted *An Enemy of the People* for Frederic March and Florence Eldredge; he reset the Norwegian scene and brought it home to Riverton, Maine, a fictionalized spa town in New England. In Miller's three-act version, moreover, "the majority is never right until it does right." But it was of course *The Crucible,* his most performed play, that gave dramatic shape to the fear, manipulation, and crass opportunism of the dangerous

McCarthyite moment—a moment that continues to haunt politics in America to this very day. No other work of American literature rivals Miller's precision in capturing the brutalizing essence of the Red Scare, when complicity was orchestrated to the naming of names before the House Committee on Un-American Activities. This was, as Lillian Hellman called it, a "scoundrel time."[4] "I have to admit," Miller said in 1989, "that it feels marvelous that McCarthy is what's-his-name while *The Crucible* is *The Crucible* still."

Even as Miller's drama turns inward to explore realities more psychological than political, as it does in *A View from the Bridge* and *After the Fall,* the consequences of his characters' actions are nevertheless developed in highly visible public domains. Eddie Carbone's unacknowledged feelings for his niece find their denouement, tragically, in full view of his Sicilian American neighbors, whose solidarity he has betrayed; Quentin's self-absorption (if that is in fact what it is) is always shadowed by an ominous watchtower. Miller's American characters are threatened with extinction, like the mustangs in *The Misfits,* the furniture once meant to last in *The Price,* or the descendants of Alexander Hamilton themselves in *The Last Yankee:* when they lose their bearings in the disappearing sense of communal identity what they have really lost is themselves. The ride down Mt. Morgan is always a one-way trip.

Seen in this light, *The American Clock,* the work Miller based in part on Studs Terkel's *Hard Times: An Oral History of the Great Depression in America,* as well as on his own family's experience, serves as both chronicle and cautionary tale. Using a frame of reference familiar to his audience from John Steinbeck's *The Grapes of Wrath,* but also from the proletarian drama of Clifford Odets, the play's epic vaudeville is set in 1929, the year of the crash. Things disappear: Lee Baum's Columbia Racer, Rose Baum's piano, Moe Baum's hope. Hard times expose the threat that was always there from the nation's very beginning: the dark underside of somebody else's newfound land. Miller's subject is, in the final analysis, America; his dramatic tableau is inspired, then transformed, by an idealism mismatched with a healthy dose of skepticism. "There's never been a society that hasn't had a clock running on it," the playwright once observed. "And you can't help wondering—how long?"

It is perhaps one of the great oddities of Miller's long career as an important American writer—one, moreover, with such vivid nativist credentials—that some of the strongest responses to his plays have consistently come from abroad. And no more so than in Britain, where, in the words of the director David Thacker, "we consider him only a little lower than Shakespeare, but a little higher than God."[5] Even in the 1970s and 1980s, when Miller's reputation was on the decline in the United States (he was dismissed by critics normally perceptive, such as Robert Brustein, as hopelessly out-of-date),[6] theaters in London and elsewhere in the United Kingdom continued to rise to the challenge of producing his work. It was during these same years that the National Theatre embarked on a highly ambitious project: making Miller an integral part of the company's repertory. Michael Rudman's revival of *Death of a Salesman,* starring Warren Mitchell, tried to bring ethnicity back into the scene by emphasizing the playwright's Jewish roots (among those who were impressed was Dustin Hoffman, who took this emphasis as inspiration for his own interpretation of Willy Loman, which was seen on American television by twenty-five million viewers). As Eddie Carbone in Alan Ayckbourn's riveting production of *A View from the Bridge,* Michael Gambon uncovered the playwright's gift for making even the most inarticulate characters eloquent. Zoë Wanamaker, sharing the Olivier stage with Tom Wilkinson, revealed a new dimension to the dynamics of *The Crucible* by locating the heartrending tragedy at the core of the Proctors' marriage: here were two vulnerable young people, both capable of loving but unable to share that love with one another. Most startling of all were two provocative British premieres: *The American Clock* and *After the Fall.* In the former Peter Wood envisioned the work as the "mural" that it was, a "story of America talking to itself." His stage solution was to let the popular music of the Depression years tell the story: "happy tunes" like "On the Sunny Side of the Street" and "I Can't Give You Anything But Love" could choreograph, then ironize, the loss of possibility and the loss of hope. And when director Michael Blakemore cast the accomplished black actress Josette Simon in the role of Maggie in *After the Fall,* this time reimagined as a sultry jazz singer, all memory of Marilyn disappeared. Icon removed, the audience at the National had the chance to experience the play as drama instead of backstage gossip.

Other British stages proved to be equally receptive to the ongoing Miller repertory. Both the Royal Shakespeare Company and the Bristol Old Vic mounted major productions of *The Archbishop's Ceiling* after the American premiere folded in Washington, DC, before reaching New York; *The Ride Down Mt. Morgan* opened not on Broadway, but on the West End; and a young cast under Paul Unwin's direction gave Miller's new version of *The Man Who Had All the Luck,* the play that closed in

New York in 1944 after only four performances, a fresh makeover in a joint venture by the Bristol Old Vic and the Young Vic in London.[7]

Something more was clearly at stake here than a few "good parts for actors."[8] The British embrace of Miller—which can be traced all the way back to Olivier's celebrated revival of *The Crucible* in the days when the National was still housed at the Old Vic on the Cut and also to Peter Brook's premiere of the revised, two-act version of *A View from the Bridge*—tells the story of a cross-cultural encounter in which theater reveals anxieties on both sides of the equation. How Miller imagines America is a topic that has been given much careful attention, yet how the British encounter with Miller comments on *both* Britain and America is an area of inquiry subject to far less scrutiny.

Socially conscious drama of the sort we associate in the United States with playwrights of the 1920s and 1930s, Elmer Rice, Sidney Kingsley, and, above all, Odets, was slow to arrive in Britain. But when it did so in the postwar period it appeared with a vengeance: no more middle-class pieties, no more cups-and-saucers. A new form of kitchen-sink drama championed by the Angry Young Men (and a few women) changed the face of British theater forever.[9] These were the same years, too, during which Miller's plays crossed the Atlantic. The compatibility of interests, not to mention the sense of dramatic purpose and style, was difficult to resist, particularly as it took shape in the work of early practitioners like John Osborne and, a generation later, in energetic young writers like David Edgar, Howard Brenton, and David Hare. The timing could not have been more perfect: Miller's drama found a place for itself on the London stage at the exact moment when Britain was beginning to have a serious moral debate with itself.

Part of that discussion, moreover, was beginning to sound increasingly American, even Milleresque, especially as the fault lines exposed in his plays became increasingly visible when staged more locally. Puritanism in Salem may have seemed like an exotic American import, but materialism and the hypocrisy surrounding it were strictly home-grown. Hard to quantify, but just as persuasive, was the growing fascination, too, with all things American, especially as personified in the tall, Lincolnesque figure who had the temerity to speak truth to power, both on and off the stage. McCarthyism made Miller something of a hero in England. The great speeches of recognition Miller provided for characters like John Proctor and Chris Keller celebrated the progressive idealism—on the one hand based on civil liberties and the right of free speech, on the other, on an individual's and a nation's power of self-correction—that made the potential of American democracy the envy of the free world in a time of the cold war. Yankee individualism, and the responsibility that came with it, mattered; Miller's drama made that point accessible. A myth, of course—but, considering the alternatives, perhaps a myth worth cultivating.

In Britain several generations of theater practitioners, skillful directors like Michael Blakemore, Paul Unwin, and David Thacker among them, helped to establish a central position for Miller on their own national stage. In doing so, they kept his repertory alive. And as committed artists often supported by a subsidized theater, their work with Miller helped them earn the right to contribute to their own national discussion without having to keep one eye permanently fixed on the box office. The playwright lived long enough to see their critical and commercial successes repeated in his own country. Beginning in the 1990s, the great revival of Miller's work moved back from Britain to Broadway. "You live long enough," the playwright once observed, "you don't rust."

The essays that follow trace the often fascinating history of Arthur Miller's theater well beyond the limits of a familiar Anglo-American vocabulary. After Shakespeare, Miller is the most produced playwright in the English-speaking world, but his drama has also achieved a remarkable degree of attention in Asia, South America, and Africa and on national stages throughout Europe. Miller quickly became an international figure with his rapid translation into other languages; but the role he plays in other cultures is by no means limited to the performance of his plays, however impressive that may be. As president of PEN (the international literary organization of poets, essayists, and novelists) Miller traveled globally, often with Harold Pinter, as a spokesperson for human rights; his advocacy brought him face-to-face with repressive regimes in Turkey, eastern Europe, and elsewhere and helped form the background for at least one new play, *The Archbishop's Ceiling*. The expansion of his dramatic perspective beyond the borders of his own country is also apparent when he writes, as he has done, about the Holocaust. Works like *Incident at Vichy* and *Playing for Time* remind his American audiences that "it" might very well "happen here"; the psychological complexity at the center of *Broken Glass* and the 1945 novel *Focus* tells us that "it" is already happening here.

But it is naturally in his relationship with the international theater community that the global range of Miller can be appreciated more fully. His most celebrated adventure in this regard has been tracked and traced in *Salesman in Beijing,* his collaborative work with his wife, the photographer Inge Morath. As part of the normalization of diplomatic relations with the People's Republic of China during the Nixon administration, Miller was invited to supervise a production of *Death of a Salesman* under the direction of Ying Ruocheng, who also translated the play. The complex cultural consequences of that production, especially from a Chinese point of view, have mostly gone unnoticed; Belinda Kong's intervention published in this collection suggests the ways in which we might begin to set that postcolonialist record straight.

Although the contributors to this volume have mostly worked on their own, I have been struck time and again when reading their essays by how often the performance history of Miller's plays on other continents coincides with moments of grim political tension—as has been the case in Spain, Argentina, South Africa, and Israel. Stage metaphor in this case welcomes political reality, reaching as it does for a dramatic through-line far beyond the specific Americanisms of the well-organized tableau. Ibsen would be pleased, as would Stanislavski; in *My Life in Art* the great Russian director remembers playing Dr. Stockmann in *An Enemy of the People,* staged in St. Petersburg soon after the massacres in Kazansky Square: "Stockman protested, Stockman told the truth [*sic*], and that was considered enough." When the audience overwhelmed Stanislavski after he recited the play's famous curtain line, "It was then I found out through my own experience what power the theatre could exercise."[10] One of the many points *Arthur Miller's Global Theater* hopes to illustrate is that there's a whole lot of Dr. Stockmann to be found, both at home and abroad, in the cross-cultural dialogue within the plays of Arthur Miller.

That dialogue continues very much into the present. Writing in the *New York Review of Books* in 2006, the Turkish novelist Orhan Pamuk, the Nobel Prize winner and his country's most celebrated author, recalled meeting Miller and Pinter in 1985 when, as copresidents of PEN, they traveled to Istanbul to support fellow writers in their fight against yet one more repressive regime. In doing so, Pamuk focused his attention on the transnational scope of Miller's work as playwright-activist. In a time of a "brutal, cruel war," he concluded by calling the dramatist, by contrast, "the pride [of] America and the West."[11]

Where Miller has *not* been performed can therefore be as telling as the international venues explored in this book. Russia, where his work suffered from two extensive periods of censorship, is a case in point. The first followed soon after the publication of his collaborative project with

Morath, called *In Russia;* the second ban was even longer, a result of the playwright's championship of free speech and the plight of Soviet Jewry. When Galina Volcheck staged *Incident at Vichy* in the 1980s, after Miller was no longer supposed to be on the index of censorship, her production was closed down. The same play faced another kind of censorship in Paris, of all places: French producers, nervous about the drama's reception in light of their country's collaboration with the Nazis in the systematic roundup of Jews, their fellow citizens, turned their back on this work. When Pierre Cardin sponsored a production of *Incident at Vichy* in Paris in the 1980s, it was spurned by critics and audiences alike.[12] All performances of Miller's work continue to be prohibited in nearly every Arab dictatorship, as well as in Iran, where it is considered subversive on the one hand and, on the other, part of the "Zionist conspiracy" of American writers of Jewish ancestry. And in India when the plays circulate at all, they do so within the retrograde Anglophile community, not within the larger culture as a whole, however fractured that may be.

When Miller does find a welcoming audience within the international theater community—and as this volume illustrates, he does so widely—his success also raises fundamental questions about transition, translation, and adaptation. What happens to the friction in a Miller work as it crosses linguistic and cultural borders? And perhaps more to the point, what does it mean for a playwright from imperial America to find a voice elsewhere, as his drama moves into some other world? Does the empire strike back, or does it remain forever trapped in the shadow Miller casts?

The contributors to this project consider such questions in a variety of ways, some more explicitly than others, and while mindful of volatile issues like cross-fertilization, hybridization, and intratextuality, they nonetheless frame their discussions within the specific and practical context of theater activity itself. The essays are divided into two related parts: the first, "Perspectives," more directly confronts dimensions of cultural transference and range, while the second, "Retrospectives," focuses attention on the implications of production history as Miller's work moves, transnationally, from one performance venue to the next. What results is a mosaic of many Millers. Invented and reinvented, the plays suddenly become "echoes down the corridor" once more, as each national theater leaves an indelible mark on his work:

> I could not imagine a theatre worth my time that did not want
> to change the world. . . .[13]

NOTES

1. Unless otherwise noted, quotations in the text from Arthur Miller are taken from my several conversations with him, beginning in 1981 and continuing through 2004. See Enoch Brater, *Arthur Miller: A Playwright's Life and Works* (London: Thames and Hudson, 2005).

2. "Stella Adler: Awake and Dream" (1989), produced by WNET for the PBS series *American Masters,* distributed by Home Vision.

3. See Enoch Brater, "A Conversation with Arthur Miller," in *Arthur Miller's America: Theater and Culture in a Time of Change,* ed. Enoch Brater (Ann Arbor: University of Michigan Press, 2005), 248.

4. Lillian Hellman, *Scoundrel Time* (New York: Little, Brown, 1976).

5. See Brater, *Arthur Miller,* 110.

6. See Martin Gottfried, *Arthur Miller: His Life and Work* (Cambridge, MA: Da Capo Press, 2003), 108, 149, 370.

7. See the chronology of Miller's premiere productions included in Gottfried, *Arthur Miller,* 449–50.

8. See Mel Gussow, "The Legacy of Arthur Miller," in Brater, *Arthur Miller's America,* 256.

9. On this point, see in particular two studies by John Russell Taylor, *Anger and After: A Guide to the New British Drama* (London: Methuen, 1962) and *The Second Wave: British Drama of the Sixties* (London: Eyre Methuen, 1971), as well as Michelene Wandor, *Look Back in Gender: Sexuality and the Family in Post-War British Drama* (London: Methuen, 1987).

10. Konstantin Stanislavski, *My Life in Art,* trans. J. J. Robbins (Cleveland: Meridian, 1956), 378–79.

11. Orhan Pamuk, "Freedom to Write," *New York Review of Books,* May 25, 2006, 6.

12. See Brater, *Arthur Miller,* 91.

13. Arthur Miller, *Timebends: A Life* (New York: Grove Press, 1987), 180.

PERSPECTIVES

Linda Ben-Zvi

Arthur Miller's Israel and
Israel's Arthur Miller

In September 1988, five months after Israel officially opened its fiftieth
year of statehood celebrations, *Ha'aretz,* the Tel Aviv–based liberal daily
newspaper, published "Waiting for the Teacher," a nineteen-stanza, free
verse poem written by Arthur Miller to mark the occasion.[1] The text
is both personal and political, brief vignettes from the writer's experiences, described in colloquial language, interspersed among longer,
lyrical passages, quasi-biblical in tone, touching on many of the themes
and concerns that have been central to Miller's theater over the same
half-century span. The poem is about Israel, but it is also about Arthur
Miller.

It begins with Miller's presentation of his credentials, a Jewish writer
addressing a Jewish country, a partisan in its history, pain, and triumph:

> I quickly understand the Jewish dead,
> Know their shock at departing alone;
> See Jewish women at the blast
> Glancing back across the centuries
> As laughter of Goyim cracks the air;
> All this I see at the gunshot.

Less automatic but also imperative is his awareness of the need to understand and acknowledge the suffering of the Palestinians, who also lay
claim to the same land:

> I have to think about the Arab dead
> Before their leaving shocks me. I must
> Instruct my heart on how they grieve.
> And stare into the centuries, hearing
> Europe's laughter and contempt.
> All this I understand when I think about it.

This kind of knowledge does not come easily, Miller acknowledges. It takes an act of will to put oneself in another's place, but the effort must be made:

> Justice must be wanted before it comes,
> Invited in from the desert
> Where it wanders about like a prophet
> Despised for his peaceful intentions
> In a time of war.
> For the heart knows its own blood best.

In the poem, Miller's "own" are Israelis. For example, he describes sharing the excitement generated on a snowy night at the Waldorf Astoria hotel in New York City, when Russian Andrei Gromeko came in from the cold, bearing the gift of public recognition for the new Jewish state. Now, it seemed "everything would change." A people who bore too long the mark of difference would be like everyone else. Miller quotes the voices dreaming of the normalcy about to happen:

> "Now there'll
> be Jewish bus drivers, Jewish cops, street
> cleaners, farmers, garbage collectors,
> prime ministers, yes even Jewish whores.
> Imagine! We'll be a normal people, an
> ordinary country like all the others."

To this list, Miller provides a coda, "And on these few sandy acres Justice done!" Justice, capitalized and all pervasive, is the rock upon which he assumes the new society will be built, its plan based on Mosaic models rather than narrowly prescribed religious practice. Thus constituted, Israel will be a nation "like any other and like none."

And what of the dream fifty years later? Tellingly, Miller shifts from prophet to playwright, invoking imagery of the theater: "The applause has died away / Dry coughs in the audience, / Dusty odor of polite boredom." The plot has gone stale, done once too often, "the one where everyone is right / and all must share the wrong." What seems to have made "the well-known loss of high expectation" more acute this time is the fact that much more had been hoped. Miller explains:

> For Israel was moral first and dreamed much,
> And now that she has merely joined the world,

A nation no different than all the rest,
The audience is reading its wrists,
While the play's antagonists repeat
The same old equality of claims.

He cites recent examples of the hatred that fanaticism has wrought, both in the Middle East and in America, enveloped in the cloak of Orthodoxy: "I have been trying these eighty years / to become an atheist, and with the help / of Orthodoxy have at last come really / close to succeeding."

And yet, it is not as simple as that. "The atheist" still finds a need to "address the Jews." The tone once more becomes personal; the pronoun of choice is first person plural.

Perhaps because we invented the promise,
and in the end it may happen that we
alone can call it finished, if so it must be.
When it becomes too easy to be a Jew it is
time to ask what has gone wrong.

Miller ends with the hope that a savior will come, not a judge to adjudicate conflicts or mete out punishment, but rather a teacher/prophet who will bring justice. Such a figure has not withheld his coming—he is not Godot—Miller emphatically states. He merely awaits the call:

For unless he is summoned
He will not come. He is unable
To idly enter the city;
Unless he is called by those who love him,
He will sit in the dust beside the gate . . .

The call for justice and compassion, issued by Miller in the poem, is the same one he delivered for over fifty years in his role as playwright/ teacher/prophet. In other writing he also positioned himself both inside and outside the gates, as actor and observer. However, what gives "Waiting for the Teacher" particular power is the fact that he draws directly from his own feelings as a Jew to deliver his message. This connection to Jewish experience is based not on religion—a "dead history," he called it[2]—nor on ethnic superiority, which has led to the sectarian divisions he describes, but rather on ethical precepts that present the doctrine "I am my brother's keeper" in the most universal sense. "Ethics, not ethnicity, became Miller's special forte," Enoch Brater rightly observes.[3] However, in the poem and in many of his other writings, there are still those compelling, sometimes inexplicable, feelings of connectedness, which have little to do with moral precepts and everything to do with common history and memories.

In his short story "I Don't Need You Anymore," his most direct critique of Jewish religious practices, his young protagonist turns his back on inherited rituals he cannot understand and refuses to practice.[4] But the adult Jew in "Monte Sant'Angelo"—the following story in the same collection—experiences a sense of pride, and even ecstasy, over his discovery of a man in a remote Italian village whom he assumes to be a Jew, someone who has somehow survived "the brainless crush of history"[5] and without even being aware is still carrying out these same traditions, whose origins he does not recognize and cannot even name. "He's Jew," the protagonist, Bernstein, is sure. His bundle metonymically marks the man. "'The way he works that bundle. It's exactly the way my father used to tie a bundle—and my grandfather. The whole history is packing bundles and getting away. Nobody else can be as tender and delicate with bundles'" (68). The implied message of the story is the need for the heart to know its own, or create its own, seeking comfort in memories of family and history, in a world of strangers.

An anecdote Miller relates in *Timebends* points to a similar need. He describes sitting in an almost empty New York subway late one evening, when a white-bearded, elderly Orthodox Jew entered, carrying, again, the "inevitable bundle wrapped in brown paper and twine." Clearly nervous, exhibiting "all the anxious energy of the survivor," the old man scanned the faces of the few in the car and made his way over to the writer, sat down, and whispered furtively in his ear: "Are you Jewish?" When Miller answered yes, he repeated the question, just to make certain. "You're Jewish?" Receiving a second confirmation, he felt sufficiently relieved to ask, "Does this stop at Canal Street?" (285–86).

What underlies the short story and the humorous scene is Miller's awareness of the powerful sway of history and shared identity, which cannot be denied, much as one might like to yank out the roots of the past. The word *goyim* is part of Miller's inherited word-hoard. In fact, what seems to distinguish him from other American writers is precisely the significance that he places on the claims of the past in the present. The same cannot be said of Miller's characters. In his theater and fiction, sons know their fathers, and they embrace them, yet they do battle with what they represent. "The job of artists," Miller has written, is "to remind people of what they have chosen to forget."[6] Here lies the nexus of the dramatic conflict, as he has defined it. If history consists of memories of the particular, how can individuals or countries ever escape the sectarian pull of "what was" as they attempt to act and react in a more humane, universal way to "what is"? "The untaught heart knows its own blood best, / but is this all the heart can know?" (5), Miller asks in "Waiting for the Teacher" and repeats in many of his plays. The question has no easy answer. A teacher/prophet may instruct about justice, as Miller tried to do in his plays by laying siege to "the fortress of unrelatedness,"[7] but the edifice is not easily breached. In addition, Miller knew that audiences had "a certain amount of resentfulness toward the presumption of any playwright to teach." Thus the "glazed glancing at watches" is a reaction courted by any playwright who dares to stage monumental confrontations in which "everyone is right / And all must share the wrong."[8]

Even were attention paid, it is not easy to convey another's pain, or to feel it oneself. Even teachers sometimes turn away. Even Jews may stand unmoved by the plight of fellow Jews, as Miller graphically displays in *Incident at Vichy* and illustrates in *Timebends,* when he describes his own inability to identify with Holocaust survivors whom he encountered during his 1948 trip to Italy, which most likely also provided the inspiration in "Monte Sant'Angelo" for Goldberg's encounter with the mythical Italian Jew. Miller had gone to a safe house in an Italian coastal town, where Jewish survivors of the death camps were gathered, waiting to escape "the graveyard of Europe forever" and go to Palestine and a new beginning. He tries to make contact with them, explaining in his pidgin Yiddish-German that he, too, is a Jew. However, this time there is no solidarity established. "They were not interested in my problem and could see no help in me for their own." Instead his gesture is met with mistrust "like acid in my face." The experience stayed with him, he explains in his autobiography, written forty years later.

> In coming years I would wonder why it never occurred to me to throw in my lot with them when they were the product of precisely the catastrophe I had in various ways given my writing life to try to prevent. To this day, thinking of them . . . I feel myself disembodied, detached, ashamed of my stupidity, my failure to recognize myself in them. (166–67)

These were not Jews carrying bundles, who could be romantically associated with images of fathers and grandfathers; these were "burnt wood, charred iron, bone with eyes"(167). No wonder the heart recoiled at their presence, as the living recoil from the dead. And yet, in Miller's moral cosmology it is these survivors of the Holocaust who stand in the inner circle next to, but not mingling with, those other specters of a private and public Jewish past: the beloved businessman father, revered religious grandfather, and Jewish patriarchs of history and folklore. To be a Jew means connection with all these avatars of Jewish experience, Miller seems to indicate, not through a bond of ethnicity as much as through a shared history, which extends beyond familial ties and includes both images of comfort as well as abhorrence. The Jew is family and memory; he is also, as Miller explains in *Incident at Vichy,* "only the name we give to that stranger, that agony we cannot feel, that death we look at like a cold abstraction."[9]

In "Waiting for the Teacher," Miller describes the special claims of Jewish identity, while at the same time arguing for the need to acknowledge the pain of others and the difficulty of doing so, even for one's "own others." It is a message that permeates all of Miller's writing. If the poem breaks no new ground in Miller studies, it does illustrate the ways in which the writer uses the case of Israel to wrestle once more with that central problem that he sees at the heart of all great theater:

> How may a man make of the outside world a home? How and in what ways must he struggle, what must he strive to change and overcome within himself and outside himself if he is to find the safety, the surroundings of love, the ease of soul, the sense of identity and honor which, evidently, all men have connected in their memories with the idea of family?[10]

If Arthur Miller found it convenient to use Israel as a way of drawing attention to the issues of family—one's own and the human family—the country has also found it convenient to use the playwright's theater as a means of waging its own battle to answer the questions, Who are we? and What do we believe? If for Miller Israel is iconic of the moral battles he needs must wage, his plays have become icons for Israelis of their own ongoing struggles with many of the same problems.

Over the last fifty years, Miller has been a constant presence in the Israeli theater, the teacher/prophet with the American Jewish accent, widely promulgated if not necessarily heeded. For him the gates have long been thrown open. After William Shakespeare and Henrik Ibsen, he is the playwright most produced in the six state-supported theaters in Israel.[11] Tennessee Williams, Samuel Beckett, and Bertolt Brecht are distant followers. There have been twenty-two major productions of his works over the past fifty years, and countless others have been presented in smaller, private venues. *Death of a Salesman* has been staged six times since its 1951 opening at Habima, Israel's national theater; *All My Sons* four times, since the original production at the Cameri Theatre in 1949; and almost all the plays written through the 1960s have been staged at least once.[12]

He is enshrined not only in the dramatic repertoire of the country but also in the educational curriculum of the state. In 1975 Israel's Department of Education replaced *Julius Caesar* with *All My Sons* as a recommended text for all secondary students electing to take the advanced English curriculum required to enter university. Although there have been other options over the years and today teachers are free to select their own plays, most still choose it. That means that for the past thirty years, most Israeli students intending to go to college have studied and been tested on *All My Sons*. For most, it is their first exposure to drama; therefore the structure of the play, as well as its themes, have had a pervasive influence on the tastes, as well as the values, of the country. Israeli audiences even today equate theater with Ibsenesque realism, popularized in the country by Miller. Equally important has been the play's impact on language acquisition. In the period leading up to the late 1960s, when virtually no English television or radio was available in Israel, the reading of English language plays in high schools provided important examples of what "good English" should be. Students learned English literary culture through Shakespeare and language skills through parsing the speeches of Marc Antony and discussing the play in English language classes. Since the mid-1970s they have discovered America through Miller and proper speech through the conversations of the Keller family, abetted now, of course, by ubiquitous American television and music. Of course, Israel is not alone in embracing Arthur Miller and his theater, but it is difficult to think of any other country—not America or even Britain—where his influence has been so pervasive for so long. It is certainly the only country to have officially institutionalized *All My Sons*.

There are several reasons to explain Miller's sustained popularity and that of his play. The most obvious would be the fact that he is a Jewish playwright speaking to a predominantly Jewish audience. But Arnold Wesker, Harold Pinter, and David Mamet are also acknowledged Jews, and they have not been able to tap the public consciousness the way Miller has. It is not just that Miller is a Jewish writer; he is a particular kind of Jewish writer, one who offers the same insistent, moral imperatives and legalistic thrust—and, at times, biblical rhythms and elevated rhetoric—reminiscent of those ancient texts sacred to the Jewish people, whose precepts shaped the State of Israel. It would be difficult to imagine Wesker, Pinter, and Mamet, except in parody, writing an essay that includes the following call to conscience:

> Let a storm come, even from God, and yet it leaves a choice with the man in the dark. He may sit eyeless, waiting for some unknown force to return him his light, or he may seek his private flame. But the choice, the choice is there. We cannot yet be tired. There is work to be done. This is no time to go to sleep.[13]

Neither would they probably conclude the introduction to their *Collected Plays* with the sentence, "If there is one unseen goal toward which every play in this book strives, it is that very discovery and its proof—that we are made and yet are more than what made us."[14] Even for secular Israelis, the message and the music of Miller, issued in such examples, strike a resonant chord that only he, of international playwrights, produces.

A second reason for Miller's great popularity and for the choice of *All My Sons* as his representative work relates to the nature of theater, as defined by the pioneers of the Hebrew stage. Nahum Zemach—the founder of Habima, the theater collective that began in Russia in 1917 under the auspices of Stanislavki's Moscow Art Theatre—was dedicated to resurrecting the Hebrew language and forging a theater that might act as a catalyst for the establishment of a new nation. Zemach argued that theater could be used as an essential tool for the realization of the Zionist Vision.[15] By the late 1940s, however, overt messages concerning the necessity for Zionism shifted to moral imperatives, particularly those touching on the individual's conscious decision to place personal wants second to the betterment of the group. Among international playwrights emerging at that time, only Miller seemed to be promulgating a similar message. Only he seemed to have a similar sense of the potential of a prophetic theater, in which a writer might stage the struggles people faced while trying to seek meaning in their personal lives and in the relationships to the general society. Of all Miller's plays, *All My Sons* was the one most directly concerned with these issues. It had been conceived originally for a prophetic theater based on the model of the Group Theatre; but as

Miller defined what constitutes a prophetic theater, it could well fit the definition of Israeli theater at the time:

> Perhaps it signifies a theater, a play, which is meant to become part of the lives of its audience—a play seriously meant for people of common sense, and relevant to both their domestic lives and their daily work, but an experience which widens their awareness of connection—the filaments to the past and the future which lie concealed in "life."[16]

Death of a Salesman, while greatly loved in Israel from the time of its first production in 1951, did not provide Israeli society with the same moral imperatives found in *All My Sons.* The program notes for the Habima production described Willy Loman as "suffering the fate of the small person being crushed by the wheels of fate."[17] Most critics assumed that he was Jewish, a shtetl immigrant plying the familiar trade of a peddler, still rootless, and still hounded, although now transported to an America that promised much but gave him little. One could cry for this unenviable situation, one critic noted; but what could one learn? Only that "Jews are always suffering," that they continue to be alienated, even in America, and that "Americans in general have a special inferiority complex. Who is not a millionaire sees himself as pitiful."[18] The remedy Miller seemed to be unconsciously offering, one critic declared, was "that Willy ought to consider moving to a society in which he could plant and find what he was looking for," in other words, Israel.[19] Willy, therefore, was not exemplary of how to live, but rather of how not to and of where not to live.

Neither was Joe Keller, but his position was assumed to be ameliorated by the idealism of Chris; and his death, unlike Willy's, was perceived as a sign that a higher moral order could be established—even in America. More importantly for Israel, the play illustrated that individuals cannot stand alone; they must consider their associations with, and responsibility to, the larger society. This message directly reflected that espoused by the new Hebrew drama, which argued that personal wants and desires must be subsumed for a greater good: the good of the new Zionist nation and of the Jewish people. Self-actualization must not overshadow societal development; personal happiness must not come at the expense of group welfare. This same message rings through *All My Sons* and explains why it, of all Miller's plays, has been most enthusiastically embraced in Israel. The work also deals with war and the terrible price that it exacts on those families and loved ones left behind, a situation Israel knows only too well.

Miller's theater in general and *All My Sons* in particular have also been embraced in Israel because they echo in their concerns and assumptions the patriarchal nature of the country and of Judaism, a religion that strictly demarcates gender, placing women in inferior positions vis-à-vis men while indicating that women are somehow responsible for male temptation and their moral lapse and fall. Similar themes are often struck in Miller's works. For a playwright who has claimed that a great theater is always based on jurisprudence and who tends to have a lawyer appear in most works, it is telling that Arthur Miller has never created a Deborah, not even a Portia. Neither has modern Israel.[20] Most of his works focus on men—sons, fathers, husbands—with women in ancillary roles. As Miller has argued, one writes what one knows:

> The man or woman who sits down to write a play, or who enters a theater to watch one, brings with him [sic] in each case a common life experience which is not suspended merely because he has turned writer or become a part of an audience. We—all of us—have a role anteceding all others: we are first sons, daughters, sisters, brothers. No play can possibly alter this given role.[21]

What Miller calls his "given role," shaped by his Jewish, first-generation, early twentieth-century upbringing, is acted out in a patriarchal script, in which his own privileged position and women's delimited "fixed roles" go unquestioned and even unrecognized. For example, when he first read Ibsen's *A Doll's House* in college, Miller noted that he could not understand why it is called a "problem" play, dealing with "the problem" of female inequality, "The women I knew about had not been even slightly unequal."[22] Clearly, when Miller writes that his theater grapples with the fundamental question of "how may a man make of the outside world a home?" the pronoun choice deliberately assumes male experience as the normative form. A similar assumption pervades Israeli religion, culture, and language. In addition, *All My Sons* bears the mark of Orthodox Judaism, with its emphasis on the generational ties between fathers and sons, in which the father enacts the ancient *Akeda*—the sacrifice of Isaac by Abraham—while a modern Sarah is helpless to stop the action and wields power only in the circumscribed arena of her garden and home, not in the public sphere, where the actions of husbands are done, he argues, for her benefit.[23] Up until recently this has been the image of the Israeli mother, expected to provide warmth and food and stand silently and helplessly grieving, while her sons went to war.[24]

A fourth reason for Miller's great appeal to Israelis is the fact that he is not only Jewish, but also American, and he has come to personify America on the Israeli stage. There are, of course, many other American playwrights produced in Israel, and some of them are Jewish—Mamet, for example—but they are of a later generation, already assimilated and no longer in direct touch with the immigrant experience, which colors Miller's theater as it does Israeli life. He is an American son of an immigrant Polish father and first-generation Polish mother, talking to a population of first-generation Israelis with similar backgrounds, who themselves became the arbiters of art and education and enshrined Miller in both spheres as the spokesperson not only for Jewish life but for the American dream. It was Miller who brought word of the *Goldene medina,* the Yiddish name for the golden land of America. The Socialist-oriented founders of Israel imagined that the new state would offer an alternative to the capitalistic model, which seemed to place love of money ahead of the common good. Yet, in practical terms, the country, which came into existence only in 1948, naturally sought to pattern itself after the strongest society in the postwar world, and that was, unquestionably, America. Ironically, Miller, the playwright who offers some of the most scathing critiques of the American dream, could also provide a vicarious glimpse into the world of power and profit many in Israel desired. At the same time, he could provide something else, which helps explain his popularity abroad. He offered his audiences a position of moral superiority, by which those equally engrossed in the same rush for riches could shake their heads in disapprobation over perceived American acquisitiveness, even as they indulged in similar rituals of materialist consumption.[25]

One final explanation for Miller's unchallenged reputation in Israel and for the importance of *All My Sons* is probably timing. The thirty-four-year-old playwright appeared on the Israeli scene at exactly the moment when the new country was searching for plays to present, particularly ones that had a strong moral message and spoke to the struggles and the experiences of present-day Jews. Few existed. Traditionally, theater had not been a Jewish medium of expression. The beginning of modern Hebrew theater had to wait until the second decade of the twentieth century, with the establishment of Habima, which attempted to forge an indigenous theater form in the Hebrew language.[26] While still in Moscow, the Biblical Studio, as the Habima was called, achieved a triumph with its production of Sholom Anski's *The Dybbuk* under the direction of Yevgeny Vakhtangov, a production that became—along with *The Golem*—a signature work when the company settled in Tel Aviv in 1931, establishing what would eventually become the national theater of Israel. In the 1940s, Habima faced the problem of mainly continuing to perform the works it had first staged fifteen years earlier; and new additions bore the performative stamp of another time and place. In response to the rigidity of Habima's cooperative structure and its acting style, a worker's theater, the Ohel (Tent Theater), emerged. This new theater staged proletarian plays such as Karel Capek's *R.U.R.* An even more ambitious theater, the Cameri (Chamber Theater) was established in 1944, declaring itself to be "a young theater for a young country," in which its actors declaimed in a Hebrew that emerged from the new Israeli culture and no longer bore Habima's Russian inflections.[27] It took the Cameri four years to produce a play that would reflect the spirit of this new beginning, which was its mandate. On May 15, 1948, the State of Israel was declared; two weeks later, as the War of Independence raged, the Cameri presented *He Walked through the Fields (Hu Halach B'sadot)* by novelist Moshe Shamir, the first play written by a native-born Israeli, which presented "in a cool, realistic manner characters and situations out of the new reality of the country."[28] Nine months later, and several days before the cease-fire that ended the fighting, Habima followed suit with Igal Mossinsohn's *In the Plains of the Negev (Be'arvoth Hanegev)*, a semidocumentary play about the siege of a kibbutz (an Israeli collective settlement) that was even then making newspaper headlines. In the same month, the Cameri staged a third war play: *All My Sons.*

It is useful to place the three plays in conjunction in order to better understand the reception first accorded to Miller's play, its subsequent absorption into the Israeli theater canon, and the ways in which *All My Sons* has become a harbinger for changing attitudes in Israeli society. On one level the three plays are similar. They all focus on young men who are called to fight in war, place private loves and desires second to the public good, and pay for their idealism with their lives or the lives of others. The sense of camaraderie that Chris Keller experiences in war and that he tries to describe to his fiancée—"they didn't die; they killed themselves for each other"[29]—lies at the center of the Israeli plays as well. However, the societies that sent these young men to war are clearly different. Both Uri in *He Walked through the Fields* and Dan in *The Plains of the Negev* are children of kibbutzim, raised in a communitarian ethos.

In these plays there are no manicured gardens that shield the inhabitants from the knowledge of war; the home front is the battlefront and all are directly at risk, not just the young defenders. Absent, too, is any note of shirking one's responsibility. When asked to join the Palmach (the army unit fighting the British and assisting illegal immigrants), Uri neither hesitates to go nor to take on the assignment of blowing up a bridge, which will certainly be a suicide mission. Neither does Dan refuse to follow the order to drive a wounded kibbutz member through the Egyptian blockade that is strangling the settlement. This is also clearly a suicide mission, one ordered by Dan's own father, the head of the kibbutz defenders, who believes that any retreat from this front line would endanger the entire country. He sacrifices his son precisely because he places the good of the group above his own personal family ties. Those women who question the sacrifice of their sons or lovers, and those neighbors who counsel retreat, eventually accept the higher pull of community and purpose that permeates kibbutz life, and by extension Israeli society at that time. Even love in these plays is described as something primarily of benefit to the group. For example, when Dan explains to his father his desire to marry, he says, "It's a whole chapter in Zionism, see? The continuity of the generations, the prolongation of the race."[30] Personal happiness, continually raised in Miller's play, is never mentioned as a competing value.

The most striking difference, of course, between the two Israeli plays and *All My Sons* is the absence in the former of the venial father, his betrayal of societal values, and the moral gulf that separates him from his sons. There are generational divides in the Israeli plays, but these arise from cultural differences: the sons are first-generation Israelis speaking a new, hybrid language the fathers and mothers cannot master and behaving in more assertive, less cultivated ways than their European forbearers. The parents may wonder about the assertiveness and pragmatism of their sons, but they clearly take pride in this new type of Jew, the sabra, who, like the fruit of the cactus, may be tough and thorny on the outside while retaining an inner sweetness. Despite these differences in language, temperament, and culture, parents and children share the same moral vision, accepting that the needs of the individual are secondary to the perpetuation of the society. The issue is not even debated within the plays and most likely not questioned by the audiences who saw them. When the sons in each of the Hebrew plays fall, little time is given to personal grief; the kibbutz quickly enshrines them in myth and song, which uplift the greater community.

Given the very American slant on the postwar themes that *All My Sons* presents, it may not be clear why Yosef Millo, the founder of the Cameri and the director of Miller's play, chose to present *All My Sons* during the same period in which the two Israeli plays were mounted, or why audiences attended despite its mixed reviews. In his program notes, Millo explained that his main purpose was "to awaken the society to the despicable nature of a war profiteer."[31] He also argued that the play provided a reminder of what could happen if they were not vigilant. "Our war is the purest of wars but still we have to look into our hearts and do an accounting so that our soldiers will not be ashamed of us" (playbill).

Critics generally followed Millo's lead, focusing on Joe Keller's selling of faulty parts and how anomalous such an act was in present-day Israel. Many also saw the play as a critique of America, or "capitalism in all its despicable shape," as the Communist daily newspaper reviewer proclaimed. Why put such people on the stage? he wondered. "Instead they should be jailed."[32] Another wrote that, while audiences can understand the anger at war profiteering and the desire of the discharged soldier for happiness, "we have no interest in the American theory of such happiness, which doesn't prevent the young man from enjoying the fruits of the comfortable life."[33] Others disapproved of what they considered the moralizing tone of the play, preferring native varieties. "We don't need an American exporting morality. For over 2,000 years we have moralized and it's become a habit with us. Therefore, I get a headache when one teacher, Rabbi Arthur Miller from Broadway, moralizes in Hebrew."[34] The same critic, however, praised the courage of the playwright and his condemnation of the American love of money. But he concluded, "It doesn't seem as if *All My Sons* are our sons, not flesh of our flesh. Here we don't commit suicide" (*Davar Weekly*).

Except for a guarded mention that Israel might also have some who profit from war at the expense of soldiers (a man had sold shoes lined with paper to the defense forces and the scandal was well known and condemned), almost to a person the reviewers touched on the theme "it can't happen here." At the same time, most mentioned how well the play was constructed and how adept the playwright was at developing characters and employing dramatic dialogue, elements that neither of the roughly written, rather simplistic local plays—for all their moral fervor—could offer. *All My Sons* clearly bore the stamp "Made in America," which was enough to guarantee respect, albeit grudgingly among some. The play ran for 57 performances, far fewer than

He Went Through the Field (171 performances), *In the Plains of the Negev* (227 performances), or the 1951 production of *Death of a Salesman* (111 performances). What is surprising is that none of the ten critics who reviewed the play discussed the ways in which Miller's call for relatedness brought it in line with Shamir's and Mossinsohn's plays. The general sense was that the middle-class world of the Kellers was so far removed from the reality of the new state at war that the play could only be appreciated as a well-told moral tale at which one shook one's head in wonder or in sorrow but not, as Millo had hoped, in recognition of what it might foretell.

This was no longer the case in 1976, when *All My Sons* was produced once more by the Cameri, directed this time by American Hy Kalus and starring the theater's leading actors, Hanna Marron as Kate and Yossi Yadin as Joe. Suddenly the play seemed all too relevant. The 1967 Six Days' War and the 1973 Yom Kippur War had radically altered the images and myths the country cherished and staged. The self-sacrificing of Uri and Dan seemed as anachronistic in the rapidly expanding consumer society as Joe Keller's actions had seemed to Israelis in 1949. In Israel in 1976, too, one could now find well-kept yards where mothers waited for their sons to return, clutching at straws and horoscopes, while the general population seemed untouched by their losses. Here, too, the home front and the battlefield were now separated by a growing abyss of indifference. Suddenly Miller's play seemed not only relevant but prophetic of what had happened in Israel in the intervening years; and it touched a deep chord of response in audiences who now flocked to see it. This production of *All My Sons* became the greatest success in Israeli theater up to that period, running for a total of 312 performances over three years in Tel Aviv and in outlying regions, small communities, kibbutzim, and army bases, to which it toured. Close to 30 percent of the population saw the play. It was still playing to full houses when the actors, claiming exhaustion, decided to close the production, despite requests that they continue.

Miller came to Israel in December 1976 and attended a special performance, flanked by Israel's then president Ephraim Katzir and then prime minister Yitzhak Rabin. Newspapers at the time reported him saying to the players, after the performance: "You made a miracle, tears came to my eyes. . . . Although I don't understand Hebrew, I see the play as I imagined it."[35] These words might be taken as a mark of Miller's politeness, meant for local consumption; however, in *Timebends* he also praises this production of *All My Sons* and explains that it provided him a new understanding of his play:

> In later years I began to think that perhaps some people had been disconcerted not by the story but by the play's implication that there could be something of a tragic nature to these recognizable suburban types, who, by extension, were capable of putting a whole world to a moral test, challenging the audience itself. This thought first crossed my mind in 1977 [*sic*] when I visited Jerusalem with my wife, Inge Morath, and saw a production of tremendous power. (135)

Miller describes the audience who "sat watching it with an intensifying terror that was quite palpable." However, at the end they did not respond as he expected. Instead of applause there was a long silence. Turning to Prime Minister Rabin, Miller asked why this had occurred, and he replied, "Because this is a problem in Israel—boys are out there day and night dying in planes and on the ground, and back here people are making a lot of money. So it might as well be an Israeli play" (135). Miller also notes that considerable credit for the impact of the play must be given to Hanna Marron, herself a victim of a terrorist act in which she lost her leg. "Perhaps it was only my imagination but her disfigurement as a result of war, which of course everyone knew about though her limp barely showed, seemed to add authenticity to Kate Keller's spiritual suffering in another war at a different time" (135). The Cameri publicity brochure for the play lists one more reason Miller gave for the overwhelming reception of his play: "Part of the success of this production I attribute to the fact that you're Jews like myself."

There were still critics in 1976 who disliked *All My Sons,* but rather than arguing that it had nothing to tell the Israeli society, several determined that the message of avarice undermining social responsibility had long since been delivered and needed no moralizing dramatic work, particularly one from abroad, to reinforce the idea. Most, however, shared the sense that what didn't work in 1949 now spoke directly to Israeli audiences, because of the rendering by Kalus and, more importantly, because of a new zeitgeist in the nation. The critic for the *Davar* newspaper summed up the feelings of many: "It's as though it's taken from the Israel experience. It makes you shiver as though the play were written here today and it hurts like a red hot iron in an open wound. It is painfully real."[36]

Since the 1976 production *All My Sons* has had two additional revivals in major theaters: in 1992 in Beersheva, directed by Itzik Weingarten, and in 1999, at the Tel Aviv Beit Lessin Theatre, directed by playwright Hillel Mittelpunkt. Both productions once more provided barometers for Israeli concerns and preoccupations at the time. In 1992 the specter of war, against which the other productions were measured, had receded, at least in public discussion. Soldiers were still dying in Lebanon, but it was a silent war, which few acknowledged at the time. More pressing was the push for private happiness, the very desire that the 1949 critics found uniquely American and not Israeli. Now Israelis sought it, too, and Weingarten's staging reflected this private need. In fact, he was praised precisely for not foregrounding issues such as moral responsibility, national loss of values, or quests for profit—by now old topics in this rapidly developing country. Instead he focused on what the country itself was increasingly seeking in its theater: personal stories in which individuals strive to find a modicum of happiness in a world that seems to thwart their desires. Whereas the family tragedy was muted in the earlier versions and in critical responses, here the personal almost totally subsumed the public. Joe's recognition of communal solidarity seemed less significant than Chris's recognition that he is finally free of the past and can start his own life with Ann. In the 1999 production, which ran in repertory through the end of 2000, Mittelpunkt followed Weingarten's lead. Despite moments in which the audience is brought into solidarity with Kate, a mother who struggles to come to terms with her son's loss—a topic that was still potent in Israel when soldiers were continuing to die in Lebanon—it seemed to be the director's intent to focus on the younger generation, who were attempting to get on with their lives. Critics of these two productions found that the play still worked, it told a good story and held the audience's attention, and it was an ideal vehicle for good actors; but none addressed any of the issues that so engaged earlier critics and audiences. The play had become a classic.

Antonin Artaud, a very different man of the theater than Arthur Miller, argued that the word "classic" was the death knell for a work: no more classics, he proclaimed. The story of Miller in Israel might bear him out. In 1999, Habima, for the first time, decided to honor one playwright in the repertoire of the year. They could have chosen Yehoshua Sobol, Hanoch Levin, or Nissim Aloni, the three great playwrights Israel has produced to date, each with a sufficient body of works to allow for such a retrospective.[37] Instead they chose Arthur Miller, perhaps in response to the recent successful stagings of several Ibsen plays at the Cameri and the revival of *All My Sons* at the Beit Lessin Theatre. It was a safe choice. Miller generally drew larger audiences than any of these local writers, at least his most famous plays did. It was, therefore, not surprising that Habima's selections were proven box office favorites in Israel: *The Crucible, A View from the Bridge,* and *Death of a Salesman* (although the last for some reason was not produced). Habima did not choose to do *The Archbishop's Ceiling, The American Clock, The Ride Down Mt. Morgan,* or *Mr. Peters' Connections* or the one-acts plays, of which only *Some Kind of Love Story* has been presented. Neither did they decide to offer *Incident at Vichy,* a Holocaust play that has never been produced in Israel, nor *After the Fall,* which has not been mounted since its 1965 premiere. Like the recent production of *All My Sons,* these revivals were faithful to the text but made no attempt to engage the moral issues that lie at the heart of the plays and might speak to a contemporary audience. They staged Arthur Miller as cultural icon, a Miller audiences have been taught to respect, certainly not the unsettling teacher/prophet with a passion for justice.

People in Israel still fill the theaters to see Miller's classics, as they do for theater in general: the country has one of the highest percentages of theater attendance in the world, with a third of the population seeing at least one play a year.[38] But what most look for is simple entertainment and a good story, not ideological debates, which were at the heart of early Israeli theater, or the prophetic theater that Miller once represented. His question posed in the poem "Waiting for the Teacher" hangs in the air: "Is this all the heart can know?" Miller may have been referring to the tendency to domesticate his work when he described "something sterile descending like a gas / Withers all vision not made of steel," something that produces "dry coughs in the audience, / Dusty odor of polite boredom" (26). He might also have been calling for a revitalized rendering of his plays when he called for the gates to be opened so that the teacher can enter, to be summoned so that he may share his message, if audiences are willing to listen. As he explains, the teacher/playwright "is unable/to idly enter the city; Unless he is called by those who love him, / He will sit in the dust beside the gate" (5).

NOTES

1. Arthur Miller, "Waiting for the Teacher," *Ha'aretz,* Magazine Section, September 25, 1998, 4–5. All excerpts of this poem come from this source. The original appeared in *Harper's* magazine, July 1, 1998.

2. Arthur Miller, *Timebends: A Life* (New York: Grove Press, 1987), 71.

3. Enoch Brater, "Ethics and Ethnicity in the Plays of Arthur Miller," in *From Hester Street to Hollywood: The Jewish-American Stage and Screen,* ed. Sarah Blacher Cohen (Bloomington: Indiana University Press, 1983), 125.

4. Arthur Miller, "I Don't Need You Anymore," in *I Don't Need You Anymore and Other Stories* (London: Penguin Books, 1969).

5. Arthur Miller, "Monte Sant'Angelo," in *I Don't Need You Anymore,* 71.

6. Arthur Miller, quoted in C. W. E. Bigsby, ed., *Arthur Miller and Company* (London: Methuen, 1990), 200.

7. Arthur Miller, "Introduction," in *Arthur Miller's Collected Plays,* vol. I (New York: Viking Press, 1957), 19.

8. Arthur Miller, quoted in *Modern Critical Interpretations of 'All My Sons,'* ed. Harold Bloom (New York: Chelsea House Publishers, 1988), 6.

9. Arthur Miller, *Incident at Vichy* (New York: Bantam Books, 1967), 105.

10. Arthur Miller, "The Family in Modern Drama," in *The Theater Essays of Arthur Miller,* ed. Robert A. Martin (London: Penguin Books, 1978), 73.

11. There are presently six public repertory theaters in Israel: the Habima National Theatre, the Cameri Theatre, and Beit Lessin Theatre, all in Tel Aviv; the Haifa Municipal Theatre; the Beersheva Municipal Theater; and the Khan Theatre in Jerusalem. To read about the particular nature of each theater and other theater venues in the country, see Shosh Avigal, "Patterns and Trends in Israeli Drama and Theater, 1948–present," in *Theater in Israel,* ed. Linda Ben-Zvi (Ann Arbor: University of Michigan Press, 1996), 9–50.

12. The Miller plays produced in Israel in the major, government-subsidized theaters include the following: *All My Sons,* 1949, 1976 (Cameri), 1992 (Beersheva), 1999 (Beit Lessin); *Death of a Salesman,* 1951, 1992, 2002 (Habima), 1967 (Zavit, no longer functioning), 1979 (Cameri), 1988 (Beersheva); *The Crucible,* 1954, 1999 (Habima), 1964 (Haifa), 1991 (Beersheva); *A View from the Bridge,* 1956, 1990, 1999 (Habima); *After the Fall,* 1965 (Cameri); *The Price,* 1968 (Cameri), 1990 (Beit Lessin); *Some Kind of Love Story,* 1991 (Khan); *The Creation of the World and Other Business,* 1994 (Haifa); *Broken Glass,* 1994 (Cameri).

13. Arthur Miller, "Many Writers: Few Plays," in Martin, *The Theater Essays of Arthur Miller,* 26.

14. Arthur Miller, "Introduction," in *Arthur Miller's Collected Plays,* 55.

15. See Freddie Rokem, "Hebrew Theater from 1889 to 1948," in Ben-Zvi, *Theater in Israel,* 51–78.

16. Arthur Miller, "Introduction," in *Arthur Miller's Collected Plays,* 16–17.

17 Program notes for Habima National Theatre's production of *Death of a Salesman* (March 4, 1951), Israel Theater Archives, Tel Aviv University The production ran for 111 performances, making it fourteenth of the fifteen longest-running plays in the Habima repertory, from 1918 to 1978. It also ushered in a series of other Miller plays, which had a great impact on Israeli theater and led to the production of other international plays, particularly those from the United States. See Emanuel Levy, *The Habima: Israel's National Theater, 1917–1977* (New York: Columbia University Press, 1979), 213–39, 293–310.

18. Review of *Death of a Salesman,* by Arthur Miller, *Al Hamishmar,* March 16, 1951.

19. Rivka Katzelnelson, review of *Death of a Salesman,* by Arthur Miller, *Davar,* March 17, 1951.

20. On women in Israeli theater, see Shosh Avigal, "Liberated Women in Israeli Theatre" and "Interview with Miriam Kainy" in Ben-Zvi, *Theater in Israel,* 303–9, 355–60.

21. Arthur Miller, "The Family in Modern Drama," in Martin, *The Theater Essays of Arthur Miller,* 81.

22. Arthur Miller, "The Shadows of the Gods," in Martin, *The Theater Essays of Arthur Miller,* 180.

23. For a discussion of Arthur Miller's plays in relation to the *Akeda,* see Shelly Regenbaum, "The Sacrifice of Isaac (The *Akeda*) and related Archetypes in Selected Works of Henrik Ibsen, Samuel Butler, Arthur Miller, Eugene O'Neill and William Faulkner," Ph.D. diss., Bar-Ilan University, Ramat-Gan, Israel, May 1978.

24. Part of the great impact of the Four Mothers Movement to Leave Lebanon, an Israeli grassroots group formed in 1997 to put the issue of Lebanon on the national agenda and to demand immediate withdrawal of Israeli soldiers, was precisely because it challenged stereotypes of mothers as passive figures, unquestioningly sending sons off to war. As one member said to me, "If God had asked Sarah if she were willing to sacrifice Isaac the answer would have been No. That was why she wasn't asked."

25. I often find that my theater students in Israel tend to accept the critiques of materialism and the failed American dream that are presented in many modern and contemporary plays and films, but they are unable to see any connections to their own society, which is equally acquisitive.

26. For the history of Habima National Theatre, in English, see Levy, *The Habima;* Mendel Kohansky, *The Hebrew Theatre* (Jerusalem: Israel Universities Press, 1969); Ben-Zvi, *Theater in Israel;* Shlomo Shva, ed., *Habima: The National Theatre Seventy Years* (Tel Aviv: Keter Publishing, 1987), which provides an album, in both English and Hebrew, of all productions in the theater's history through 1987.

27. Levy, Kohansky, and Ben-Zvi also provide material on the Cameri Theatre in Ben-Zvi, *Theater in Israel.*

28. Quoted in Mendel Kohansky, *The Hebrew Theatre* (New York: Ktav, 1969), 154.

29. Arthur Miller, *All My Sons,* in *Arthur Miller's Collected Plays,* vol. 1 (New York: Viking Press, 1957), 85.

30. Igal Mossinsohn, *In the Plains of the Negev (Be'arvoth Hanegev)* (1949), playscript, trans. Reuben Avinoam, Theater Archives, Tel Aviv University, vol. 27.

31. Joseph Millo, program notes for playbill of *All My Sons* (1948–49), Israel Theater Archives, Tel Aviv University.

32. Yitzchak Hirshberg, review of *All My Sons,* by Arthur Miller, *Kol Ha'am,* March 4, 1949.

33. Y. Zisman, review of *All My Sons,* by Arthur Miller, *Davar,* March 4, 1974.

34. Y. M. Neeman, review of *All My Sons,* by Arthur Miller, *Davar Weekly,* March 3, 1949.

35. Arthur Miller, quoted in publicity playbill, *All My Sons,* Israel Theater Archives, Tel Aviv University.

36. Yoel Nir, review of *All My Sons,* by Arthur Miller, *Davar,* February 25, 1976.

37. For studies of the theater work of Nassim Aloni, Yehoshua Sobol, and Hanoch Levin see Ben-Zvi, *Theater in Israel.*

38. For a study of Israeli theatergoing habits and the subjects presented, see Shoshana Weitz, "From Combative to Bourgeois Theater: Public Theater in Israel: 1990," in Ben-Zvi, *Theater in Israel,* 101–16.

Belinda Kong

Traveling Man, Traveling Culture
Death of a Salesman and Post-Mao
Chinese Theater

That the 1983 Chinese production of *Death of a Salesman,* staged by the
Beijing People's Art Theater under the direction of Arthur Miller himself, marks a significant moment of Sino-American cross-cultural collaboration is not to be doubted. However, the nature and direction of
significance do not always correspond with the way previous accounts
(including Miller's own) have imagined it. This episode of "crossing"
is, first and foremost, not a triumph of American literature or evidence
of some common human spirit, but a distinctly Chinese event: It cannot be understood apart from the specific historical struggle between
Chinese artist-intellectuals and the Communist Party leadership. Toward
this end, I will investigate Miller's role in the episode within a larger narrative of Maoist and post-Mao China's negotiations with Western cultural imports. My main focus is thus on the cultural-political dimensions
of the *Salesman* production as they emerge within Chinese contexts.
Methodologically, then, this essay aims to foreground the possible self-
sufficiency of non-Western contexts and also the prospect that, within
these discourses, the American reference can sometimes occupy only a
place at the margin.

Preludes: Of Texts and Contexts

They're really coming out of a cave and blinking their eyes. (Arthur Miller,
in reference to the Chinese people)[1]

I sense something wild about the audience, something untamed, avid, and,
for want of a better word, uncultivated. (Arthur Miller, in reference to the
Chinese audience during the premiere of *Death of a Salesman* in Beijing)[2]

I'm relying upon my convictions that I have the right to ask of these
Chinese actors that they be as Chinese as they know how and to feel as

> Chinese as they feel. If their acting is profound enough in its rendering of human relations, you will have a reality up there that will transcend the national culture. (Arthur Miller, in reference to the cast in Beijing)[3]

> But it suddenly seemed to me that with all their progress they were still being actors rather than humans who were privileged to express a poetic vision that lies within the play. (Arthur Miller, in reference to the Chinese actors staging *Death of a Salesman*)[4]

In this late age of our developed critical discourses, given the heterogeneous theoretical typographies over which we as critics necessarily traverse, it is perhaps thankfully impossible for us to read the previous lines without appreciating the relevance of a postcolonial critique. The resonant continuity of an imperialist discourse in Miller's rhetoric brings only too readily to mind Edward Said's argument about Orientalism, namely, that it is the West's way of restructuring, knowing, and domesticating an entire hemispheric space summarily labeled "the Orient."[5] The metaphor of China as a cultural cave; the portrait of the Chinese people as "untamed" and "uncultivated" cultural barbarians, or alternately, as mindless mimics of a mode of being not their own; the belief that the Western artist turned cultural hero possesses the "poetic vision" of a transcendental and universal humanity that can liberate the simple-minded from their ideological delusions; and the rather too unsubtle colonialist trope of "getting China territory"—all these expressions find plentiful and uncomfortable echoes in *Orientalism*.

In the same circumstance, however, there is always the task of negotiating a general theoretical framework on the one hand and the particularity of a cultural practice on the other, without wholly collapsing one under the other's power. In this instance, the practice concerned is Miller's 1983 production of *Death of a Salesman* in Beijing, mounted by the Beijing People's Art Theater. Despite the remarkable traces of imperialist rhetoric previously noted, it is perhaps equally vital to recognize the lack of any imperialist *designs* on the writer's part. Here we have a peculiar manifestation of the colonizing mentality, which continues to shape the narrativization of history even in the absence of colonizing impulses. To be sure, this ironic disjunction between language and intention throws into uneasy relief the immediate appropriateness of a postcolonial critique—that is, something along the line that Miller's play serves as an ideological tool of American cultural hegemony over the Chinese mind. We have reached, maybe, a point of theoretical saturation and dubiety where it is neither intellectually obligatory nor revealing to read every cross-cultural venture between East and West as invariably complicit in a larger imperialist project. And it more than deserves noting that, to Miller's credit, this singularly formidable endeavor at cross-cultural exchange was performed with visible success, without abortive interventions by either government, without the punctuation of violent resistance, and to the satisfaction of both sides involved.[6] Against the perceived barrier of an absolute and insurmountable cultural relativism on the one hand, and the theoretical dilemma of an inescapable hegemonic reinscription on the other, the Beijing *Salesman* continues to hold out the possibility of nonviolent contact and mutually respectful dialogue.[7]

Moreover, in the act of negotiating theory and practice, we face a simultaneous task of reconstructing the event itself, which directs us to the multiple and often incommensurable points of view from which history can be, and ideally is, narrated. The problem here is exacerbated by a terrific dearth of published material, both primary and secondary, concerning the episode. Given that the only full-length text on this event is *Salesman in Beijing,* Miller's own journal-log of his trip, it is neither incidental nor surprising that subsequent commentaries and scholarship, using his account as their base text, go on to reduplicate, reaffirm, and recirculate certain structural attitudes of a complacently ethnocentric and culturally myopic stripe.

One may take as an exemplary instance Brenda Murphy's book *Miller: Death of a Salesman* (1995).[8] With most of the source accounts and reviews employing an imperialist rhetoric concerning the Beijing *Salesman,* it does not altogether astonish us that Murphy therefore also feels authorized to write, with neither scruples nor aversion, of the "simplistic aesthetics" of the Chinese and their addictive need for ideological didacticism. Even while observing, quite correctly, that "an anti-Maoist sentiment at the heart of Chinese culture . . . persisted despite all the leveling efforts of fifty years of Communist rule," Murphy intimates that the Chinese were not themselves aware of their discontent until Miller came to release and illuminate it. Reading through and with the lens of Miller's journal, her narrative dutifully distills his most self-aggrandizing moments and condenses them into an occidental teleology, whereby *Salesman* is at last triumphantly declared to have transcended "the ethnic question" and "the ethnic consciousness that had constrained both [his] and the actors' conception of the play."[9] In this claim for Miller's universal liberating powers, we detect once more an unwitting revival of the imperialist narrative. It is all too appropriate and telling, then, that Murphy's discussion of the Beijing production is embedded within a larger section on foreign performances of the play, as if to signal *Salesman*'s ability to travel anywhere and everywhere while spreading sweetness and light like an incarnation of Arnoldian culture. One need not be well versed, or otherwise very much invested, in the intricacies of postcolonial theory to desire some troubling and ruffling of this too casually authoritative pose.

Since what remains consistently elided in this too uniform and one-sided narrative is an informed consideration of the Chinese perspective(s), this essay aims precisely to recontextualize the Beijing *Salesman* within intersections of contemporary Chinese history, politics, and theater. The Beijing *Salesman* is first and foremost a Chinese event, and, more spectacularly, it is but one act in a lived national drama, staged between artist-intellectuals and party leaders, begun long before Miller's arrival. I offer this counternarrative as neither a sub-version nor a *sub-version* of the American one, but as the story already available to and told by those familiar with the Chinese contexts. Perchance, too, a small step may consequently be taken toward the opening, or the threshold, of *our* cultural cave.

How It Happened: The Sense of a Beginning

> The beginning, then, is the first step in the intentional production of meaning.[10]

By virtue of its dual national origins, an enterprise such as the Beijing *Salesman* tends to bifurcate retellings along cultural lines, rendering problematic any attempt at locating a single, focused beginning. In consequence, too, the different specifications of a beginning reproduced significantly opposing emphases and meanings. Most directly available in this respect are Miller's introductory remarks in *Salesman in Beijing* as to "How It Happened," where he locates the relevant moment of beginning, somewhat dramatically, in the arrival of his own person. His invitation to China is therefore cast as a genesis in two senses, aesthetic and pedagogical:

> In that short period [1979 to 1983] they [the Chinese theatrical company] had come to realize that with China's near opening to the West the audience might conceivably have become sophisticated enough to follow *Salesman,* whose style was entirely innovative for them. Besides, by the early 1980s a small but significant number of new Chinese plays had been written

and performed in a style much like that of *All My Sons*, which observes the structure of the classic realist play and would thus have little to teach them about new forms.

What still remained in great doubt was whether they could mount *Salesman* without outside help, and this finally led them to insist I come to China to direct it.[11]

Confronted with the artistic backwardness of a propaganda-driven post-Mao theater, Miller sees his role as that of artistic teacher and liberator, a self-estimation happily gratified when, shortly after his arrival, the troupe of Chinese actors conferred upon him the title of "Foreign Expert." From the first, Miller's narrative casts the difficulty of staging his play in strictly technical and formal terms: He comes to China in order to teach the Chinese "new forms" of drama and the methods of staging these and he possesses knowledge that the Chinese collectively lack. To be sure, one can discern some disturbing Orientalist accents in this comfortable dichotomy of knowledge between West (has) and East (has not). Such paternalistic portioning of privilege also certainly makes less threatening what is otherwise told as a highly unsettling journey, with something in the vein of a "stranger in a strange land" motif, though attended by some perhaps too unembarrassed tropes of Oriental dirt, poverty, and inscrutability. Hence we read in the first log entry of *Salesman in Beijing:*

> Like Prague, Beijing burns soft coal and cooks on charcoal; thus the air is haloed with dust and shoes are never clean. But here they also have sand blowing in from the Gobi desert. Bronchitis is the common ailment. I had almost forgotten how poor they are and as grayly dressed as their city. . . . One has only their controlled expressions to go by; I am like a deaf man searching their eyes for emotions, which finally I cannot read.[12]

Miller's narrative delicately finds its counterplot in John Woodruff's, which felicitously gives us more than the sense of a cultural vacuum in post-Mao China:

> The screening committee of the People's Art Theater, which is the experimental company at Capital Theater, Beijing's main resident acting house, initially turned *Bus Stop* down in 1982 on grounds that its technique was too avant-garde for Beijing's audiences to understand. So Gao Hangjian [Gao Xingjian], the

playwright who wrote it, and Lin Zhaohua, a director who wanted to stage it, devised a plan to introduce contemporary Western-style drama to Beijing audiences. They started by staging, in 1983, a politically inoffensive modernist piece called *Warning Signal,* written by Gao specifically for the purpose. . . .

About the time *Warning Signal* was to move to the main stage, I interviewed Lin Zhaohua, the director. He told me that the next step in introducing modernist drama would be to bring Arthur Miller . . . to Beijing to direct a production of *The Death of a Salesman.* Mr. Miller's play filled the main house of Capital Theater for several weeks, to enthusiastic reviews from newspapers and broadcasters. Then, Mr. Lin and Mr. Gao tried again with *Bus Stop.* But even after all the preparations, the play closed without explanation after a few little theater performances and never did have its scheduled main stage run.[13]

With brisk suggestiveness, Woodruff locates the beginning of the Beijing *Salesman,* its cause of emergence and raison d'être, in theatrical activities initiated prior to Miller's arrival, whose presence is then recast, somewhat less heroically, as "preparation," a stepping-stone for the more experimental drama then being written by Chinese playwrights. The specific circumstances to which Woodruff refers—the controversy surrounding Gao Xingjian's play *The Bus Stop*—anticipates a later section of this essay. For now, we take from Woodruff's account the implication that, first, dramatic activities in China intersected significantly with extradramatic forces, and second, the Beijing *Salesman* was part of an attempt by certain Chinese artist-intellectuals to navigate dangerous political waters.

Here it may be instructive to review in synoptic form the events in the history of the People's Republic of China (PRC) that bear fundamental pertinence to the theatrical situation of the early 1980s. There are less fitting places to start than Mao's 1942 "Talks at the Yan'an Forum on Art and Literature." Of Communist notoriety, "Mao's Talks," given at the height of the Sino-Japanese War, early on defined the literary policy that the Communist Party would pursue in later years: while it was acknowledged that literary works could be evaluated by both artistic and political criteria, the latter acquired not only emphasis but primacy.[14] Drama in particular was entrusted with a vital ideological role. With the encouragement of the party, an extensive network of amateur drama groups developed at the local level, giving frequent village performances on such contemporary matters as farm productivity, army-civilian relations, and self-defense strategies against enemy attacks. Full-length productions unrelated to the war were variously criticized and aborted.[15] As it so happened that the civil war between Communists and Nationalists picked up quite exactly where the Sino-Japanese conflict ended, drama continued to serve highly politicized and militarized functions. Very justly, then, has the theatrical scene of these constitutive PRC years been called "a drama born and nurtured in revolution and wars."[16]

Less romantically grandiose was the use of theater for ideological feuds and indoctrination during the Cultural Revolution (1966–76). Jiang Qing (a.k.a. Madame Mao) famously and fiercely led the way by laying down some stern prescriptions on the ideological content of dramatic productions. It thus came to be that the "model play" was to contain "Three Prominences": Not simply were writers to create only proletariat heroes, but among all the characters, prominence was to be given first to the positive characters, then to the heroic characters among the positive ones, and finally to the principal hero among all others. This formula was to be coupled with the "Three Unities," according to which "the leaders supply the thought, the masses supply the life experiences, and the writer supplies the techniques."[17] Amateur theater groups were once more employed to "propagate Marxism, Leninism, and Mao Zedong thought to the people, to carry out the educational goals on the ideological and political battlefront, to coordinate closely with the actual struggles and to serve the great revolutionary movements."[18] These prescriptions bred a theater of correct heroization and perfect poetic—which became no longer separable from ideological—justice. Ironically, the very group of people responsible for this cultural tyranny, the so-called Gang of Four and their associates, were for the most part themselves literary critics and, like Jiang Qing herself, theatrical performers. There were none who could do a better or more thorough job of collapsing drama into pedagogy and discipline than those who knew well from professional experience the ideological power of the theater.

Meanwhile, it was with an almost fateful predictiveness that Socialist realism became the dominant literary model. Of Stalinist Soviet origins, it entered into Maoist China and encountered its due measure of modification. It emphasized, on the one hand, the positive aspects of Socialist labor and, on the other, the representation of such in transparent "realist" terms, which more often than not entailed hyperbolic heroes and villains. Were it not for historical hindsight, perhaps much can be said, along Marxian lines, for Socialist realism's aim to demystify and popularize what had been an elitist artistic tradition, or, more specifically along Lukacsian lines, for the commitment of its fictional form to Socialist possibilities. Alas, the practical fulfillment of a totally politicized art, certainly approximated if not entirely accomplished during the Cultural Revolution, while *theoretically* promising as a form of social responsibility, left something to be desired by those who were required to abide by its strictures. If Lu Xun is often held as the father of modern Chinese literature in precisely this sense—that is, as the writer who initiated the tradition of literature as political voice of the people—it falls on Gao Xingjian, a playwright half a century later in post-Mao China, to lament in retrospect that "it was a misfortune for literature that the writer Lu Xun was crushed to death by the politician Lu Xun."[19]

In sum, we may observe that, in those years of the Cultural Revolution, it was not so much that creative activities ceased altogether, but rather that art as a field of cultural production lost its autonomy and became an inflated form of national governance, a mechanism of social control and discipline.

Yet the greater the bureaucratic control over artistic practices, the more intense the intellectual resistance against ideological reduction. It was precisely due to this high-handed governance of the artistic field that artistic autonomy became a locus of contestation of various acts of refusal and retrieval. And it was precisely in this contest over autonomy that the artistic field became an arena where battles over the degree of intersection between aesthetics and politics were waged, certainly between intellectuals and party leaders; but since these two categories often overlapped to some extent, the struggle was also at times internal to the party leadership itself. For instance, as early as 1957, in the aftermath of an anti-Rightist movement and the "million poems campaign," which demanded works with "happy peasants singing folk songs," intellectuals expressed criticisms of political excesses through diversely veiled writings. Even Tian Han, a playwright who had himself been put in charge of the anti-Rightist movement, fretted about the crudity to which literature was reduced and duly responded with a military allegory critiquing the Maoist regime.[20] Again, in 1962, in reaction to the radical Cultural Revolutionists' attempts to dictate dramatic practice, which included the cancellation of all drama theory courses and the elimination of all Western plays from the national dramatic repertory, moderate party officials and intellectuals convened at the All China Forum on the Writing of Spoken Drama, Opera, and Children's Plays in order to protest ideological control of the theater. Prominently featured was General Chen

Yi, who spoke for the necessity of creative autonomy and individuality.[21] And even more immediately preceding Miller's arrival, in the first few years following Mao's death in 1976, the period of "liberating the mind" saw the emergence of a "literature of the wounded" that explored and exposed the physical and psychological trauma of the Cultural Revolution. A multitude of plays in this genre bitterly condemned the Gang of Four, invoking a nostalgia for the early years of the PRC when Communism had once seemed the utopian answer to national chaos.[22] Yet even in this period of possible criticism, only certain targets of the past were officially sanctioned for denunciation. Among those writers who contested the limits of political critique was Wang Ruowang, who, in a daring inversion of the earlier Maoist principle of political priority, declared that politics was not subservient to literature but was instead its "younger brother."[23]

It was therefore very much the case that, even from the beginning of PRC history, the artistic field was far from homogeneous or stable. It often served as the stage for conflicts where the distinguishing (battle) lines between ideology and critique, politics and art were continually fought over and redrawn. Miller's presence was not the issue that shook the Chinese mind from its ideological slumber, for the critical orientation had been a long and arduously intimate, if sometimes costly, tradition. Indeed, one comes to think that this struggle for expressive freedom in contemporary China reveals, in an amply grounded manner, an interplay between power and resistance that Michel Foucault would have appreciated.

Western Imports: The Entrance of/into (a Late-Coming) Modernism

It [*Death of a Salesman*] can really open the world repertory to China, not merely as a curiosity, but as an experience in which they can participate, and one that would do much to penetrate their isolation as a culture, a major accomplishment whose resonances can roll out in many surprising directions. (Arthur Miller)[24]

Wilder's *Our Town* came relatively late in the Chinese theatrical scene, when audiences had already been flooded with an overdose of Western plays. . . . Japanese, Indian, Soviet, Greek, French, and East European dramas were also performed in this period. Indeed, perhaps no other modern country has witnessed such a great number of foreign plays passing into its national dramatic repertory in such a few years. (Xiaomei Chen)[25]

If it is quite a settled thing, then, that the moment of beginning relevant to our analysis rests in some time prior to Miller's arrival in Beijing, it may be said with equal assurance that Miller's role was somewhat less impressive than that of the original Western cultural avatar. Certainly, the two years following Mao's death and the arrest of the Gang of Four in 1976, which decisively ended the decade-long Cultural Revolution, saw much confusion within the party itself. However, the next few years of the post-1978 situation saw, by contrast, the consolidation of Deng Xiaoping's power and his active promotion of modernization policies. The drive to modernize was fervently carried out on multiple fronts, with the cultural one advancing concurrently with, if not always so consistently sanctioned as, the economic. It was thus into an atmosphere of great creative energy that all things Western, whether technological or artistic, material or intellectual, initially entered. To the excitement of intellectuals in particular, the new constitution of 1978 promised as one of the "four big freedoms" that of expression. Consequently, numerous new genres of writing arose, including the aforementioned "literature of the wounded," as well as, among others, a new variety of critical fiction and a new mode of poetry called *menglong,* consciously styled after the modernist poetics of Ezra Pound and T. S. Eliot.[26]

Meanwhile, Western imports also came in the form of what Chinese intellectuals were then calling "New Theory." As has been discussed elsewhere, "in the early 1980s the names of Habermas, Derrida, Foucault were suddenly familiar to Chinese intellectuals, along with those of other Western writers and thinkers who had been banned for half a century."[27] This New Theory included everything from new criticism to reader's response, structuralism and semiotics to post-structuralism and deconstruction, psychoanalysis to feminism and cultural studies. Xiaobing Tang, one such intellectual who became a student of the New Theory, has remarked on the voracious rapidity with which the "entire course of literary criticism of the twentieth-century West and more [was] frantically crammed into scores of introductory essays, dozens of translated selections, all in a manner of a few years." And it is with great retrospective acumen that Tang attributes this eager embrace of Western theory to the "general intellectual effort to translate the text of contemporary China into a supposedly world language."[28] In other words, the routes and value of cultural transmission were not taken to be unilateral; quite the contrary, imported Western thought served very specific national goals in that, ideally, it was to supply the formative grammar for a reverse translation that would permit China to gain access into, while making itself intelligible to, the rest of the world.

So it was in company with a host of Western theories that translations of Western literature found its audience. In regard to the theater, studies of contemporary Western drama began to appear as early as 1978, when literary historian Zhu Hong published a critical survey of the theater of the absurd alongside a translation of Pinter's *The Birthday Party*. The year 1980 further saw the publication of two anthologies: the first, a collection of absurdist plays, brought together Samuel Beckett's *Waiting for Godot,* Eugène Ionesco's *Amedée, or How to Get Rid of It,* Edward Albee's *The Zoo Story,* and Harold Pinter's *The Dumb Waiter;* the second, a more general collection of modernist works, included such expressionist plays as August Strindberg's *The Ghost Sonata,* Georg Kaiser's *From Morn to Midnight,* Ernst Toller's *Masses and Man,* and Eugene O'Neill's *The Hairy Ape,* with Jean-Paul Sartre's *Morts sans sépulture* joining the ranks in the second volume, published the following year.[29]

Thus it was that, by 1982, Western plays of the most (post)modernist stripe were becoming familiar to the Chinese intellectual readership. And it was not entirely incidental that existentialist drama, with its thematizing of modern alienation and its formal experimentalism, stimulated especial interest in a younger generation of playwrights coming to artistic maturity in the immediate wake of the Cultural Revolution. On the one hand, they sought new dramatic forms at a time when aesthetic autonomy and creative individuality, revoked and contested for decades, were finally regarded as a real possibility in the era of liberalization. They also recognized in the motifs of existential inertia a forceful resonance with the national experience during the Cultural Revolution. Both formally and thematically, existential theater found a ready and sympathetic afterlife in the post-Mao context.

Of most relevant consequence in this respect is Gao Xingjian's *The Bus Stop (Chezhan),* written in 1982.[30] Sometimes referred to as the first Chinese absurdist play and often compared to *Waiting for Godot,*[31] the play consists of a group of passengers, simply and generically identified, though with more definite social markers than Beckett's Vladimir and Estragon, as Old Man, Girl, Hothead, Glasses, Mother, Carpenter, and Director Ma. In palpably absurd fashion, they queue up to wait for a bus that passes many times before them but that never stops. Their ensuing complaints about the transportation service and other dysfunctional systems, while touching on some genuine social problems of the period, would occasionally break down into unintelligible chatter rather than culminate in a sustained critique. On this note, one of Gao's suggestions for the play indicates that "the dialogue is at times clear and direct, and at other times vague or even devoid of meaning, or is uttered simply for the sake of talking—like waiting for the bus without knowing why."[32] At moments, too, a character may drop a remark of amazing and almost metatheatrical lucidity, as when Old Man, "suddenly becoming very old and decrepit," bemoans the outrageousness of "making passengers stand around and wait till their hair turns grey. Absurd . . . really absurd."[33] For it as at this point that Glasses looks at his watch and announces in shock that ten years have passed. The play ends with the seven actors stepping out of their roles and puzzling aloud simultaneously, in what Gao calls a "polyphonic dialogue," as to why the yet-seated audience does not leave. This metadramatic turn displaces the theme of waiting onto the audience itself, and the ten-year period of stasis within the play likewise becomes an allegory for the Cultural Revolution decade, which, to many in the audience as well, had promised much progress but yielded merely empty time. Very pointedly, then, Gao orients his play as a rendition of contemporary Chinese social experience rather than, as sometimes held by both his detractors and admirers, as an existentialist comment on some universal human condition.

That Gao ran into trouble as soon as he tried to put his play on the stage is a matter that deserves examination. We may recall here Woodruff's remarks regarding its initial rejection: The Beijing People's Art Theater—the same company that produced *Death of a Salesman* just one month before staging *The Bus Stop*—had ostensibly expressed concern that Gao's play was too technically avant-garde; hence the necessity of first mounting a less experimental piece like Miller's. Indeed, despite what Xiaomei Chen has called "an overdose of Western plays" flooding Chinese theaters in the early 1980s, most of these were far less experimental than *The Bus Stop*. These were plays in the more classic realist tradition by Henrik Ibsen and Anton Chekhov, but also by the mature Eugene O'Neill. Of particular popularity was William Shakespeare, so that just a few years witnessed, among others, *Macbeth* (1980), *Romeo and Juliet* (1981), *The Merchant of Venice* (1981), *King Lear* (1982), and *Othello* (1983);[34] the pattern was to culminate in a general Shakespeare festival in 1986, when twenty-six Shakespearean plays were produced in multiple dialects and dramatic modes.[35] More unconventional productions included Bertolt Brecht's *Life of Galileo* (1979), but then Brecht had always been favorably received in the PRC due to his Marxist background and his acknowledged inspiration by, and borrowings of, traditional Chinese theater. The foreign plays produced in this period were not so formally adventurous, then, or as capable of stretching the boundaries of contemporary Chinese theater, as Gao and some of his fellow playwrights would have it.

Yet the terms in which Gao was subsequently attacked, even months after the abrupt cancellation of his play, indicates that objections were more than merely technical. To be sure, works such as *Macbeth* and *The Life of Galileo* were eminently interpretable as allegories of the Maoist regime, albeit not as incisive a one as *The Bus Stop*. What strictly set Gao's play apart was its peculiar combination of modernist aesthetics and political criticism—as embodied in the work of a *Chinese* playwright. He Wen, one of the first critics to make that apt, if obvious, comparison between *The Bus Stop* and *Waiting for Godot,* in fact did so in order to condemn Gao's "blind worship" and "mechanical copying" of Beckett, who was in turn castigated as epitomizing capitalist "idealism" and "nihilism."[36] He Wen criticized Gao's play not only for its pessimism but also for its historical "distortions," particularly its depiction of the "futility of waiting," which was construed as a denial of Socialist progress and of the possibility of remedying contemporary problems. Insofar as the play's dramatizing of inertia and communicative collapse was read as a false ontology that renounced Socialist struggle and utopian possibilities, He Wen in effect projected onto Western modernist *form* an immanent, anti-Socialist ideological *content*. Such a view was echoed by Xi Yan, who assailed Gao's modernism as a "crisis of faith" and an "erroneous trend of thought."[37] In this instance, the problem with Western modernism seemed not so much to proceed from a fear of potential interpretive density or elitism, since Gao's play aroused anxieties precisely because it was so abundantly transparent. Rather, the vexation involved the appropriation of Western modernist form for purposes of ideological "deviation" or opposition. Only too plainly had Gao pressed the formal experimentalism of European absurd theater into the service of an anti-Maoist political critique. He Wen's comments implied that, had Gao cast his criticism in a more familiar mode such as Socialist realism, the play would have met with less disapproval because it would have been more "native" to the Chinese theater. That Gao had actually prefaced *The Bus Stop* with a one-scene play by Lu Xun did not save him from the accusation that he was aligning himself with an earlier critical realist tradition—for "how can we put a lonely, arrogant individualist who sets himself above the masses on a par with an indomitable revolutionary?"[38]

Evidently, then, the import of and engagement with Western theatrical conventions would not work naively or neutrally. Xiaomei Chen has argued insistently and persuasively that, in contemporary China, all things associated with the West carried what Pierre Bourdieu would call "cultural capital," both for party leaders and for intellectuals. The intended signifying content of this capital, however, was often distinctly different for each group: as the official Maoist line had long evoked the image of the West as a negative other, post-Mao appropriations of Western artistic forms effectively constituted a counterdiscourse, insofar that "any Western play on stage was itself a form of political discourse directed against the previous regime."[39] Or, in other terms, Western imports can be understood to operate within a field of cultural politics that in part aimed to "demarginalize the local center."[40] Singularly instrumental in this endeavor, too, was the New Theory, which "progressively assisted in the process of 'deconstructing' the tenacious hold of intellectual habits which became entrenched, reinforced and established as tradition during the Cultural Revolution."[41] Thus conceived, the translation of Western works provided both vocabulary and grammatical structure not only for official modernizing objectives but also for unofficial internal critiques.

It must be recognized, then, that any sustained use of Western conventions in post-Mao China trod a fine ideological line between collaboration and resistance. Even with the opened space for artistic innovation in the liberalization era, the cultural subversiveness conservatives always uneasily attached to all things Western, especially to modernist forms, left artist-intellectuals limited room for maneuver. As already observed, He Wen's denunciation of *The Bus Stop* evinced a worry that the use of Western cultural imports signified not just aesthetic newness but ideological defection from Socialism or subservience to bourgeois capitalism. The fear, a general one among the rearguard-minded, was that, in adapting and propagating the most experimental Western techniques, Chinese artist-intellectuals, and playwrights in particular, were irresponsibly exposing audiences to the harmful mesmeric effects of foreign hegemonic forces. In other words, they were presumably committing an unwitting act of self-imperialism. He Wen is again instructive and exemplary in this regard when he accused "some comrades" of planning to "transplant" indiscriminately the entire world outlook and artistic philosophy of the modernist school to China, and use it to serve as the "guiding ideology."[42] And it was in similarly apprehensive terms that the deputy head of the Propaganda Department dubbed *The Bus Stop* "the most poisonous play written since the establishment of the People's Republic."[43]

It may not be tangential to note here some points of disconnection from an academic perspective. It is certainly a matter of some irony that the customary postcolonial critique—that is, something along Saidian lines as to the totalizing power of Western discourses, even among the colonized—replicates fairly exactly in post-Mao contexts the logic of an authoritarian regime in its continual business of maintaining ideological control at home. However, in point of fact, fashionable theories notwithstanding, China was, as has been said elsewhere, "only obsessed with itself."[44] At least in the early 1980s, Chinese intellectuals clearly felt it more urgent to establish domestic lines of definition and opposition before venturing onto more international ones; the possibility of Western cultural imperialism was not given serious consideration until the late 1980s, after about a decade of global cultural negotiations. It is in this light that we can understand why a paradigmatically Western play like *Death of a Salesman*—with its narrative of the dislocated common man, rejected by and ejected from both the capitalist machinery and the American dream—would encounter no hindrance from the ever-wary ideological watchdogs, while *The Bus Stop,* also about those who have been "cast aside by life and forgotten by the world,"[45] would by contrast be hounded with relentless fury. Whereas the former play dramatized, with welcome ideological appropriateness, the failure of an imperial other's ideals, the latter quite saucily turned that other's formal methods into a critique of one's own national leaders. If the threat of Western cultural imperialism was depreciated by intellectuals at this point, it was always very much on the minds of conservative cultural guardians.

In fact, He Wen's attack of Gao came precisely amid an "anti-spiritual pollution campaign," launched in October 1983 by Deng Xiaoping.[46] After consolidating his power in 1982, Deng reverted from his initial stand of liberalization back into cultural traditionalism and conservatism. The 1983 campaign was an extended conservative reaction on Deng's part to the intellectual debate, begun earlier that year and pursued too vigorously for his tastes, regarding the existence of alienation in contemporary Chinese society, in effect using Marxist categories to analyze Maoist and post-Maoist Socialism. To suppress rising political criticism and tighten ideological discipline, Deng urged campaign heads to expand their censure from those who debated alienation to, among others, those who advocated modernist over realist literature. Gao, who had been under surveillance since 1981, when his pioneering book on modern fiction was published, became an easily available target—particularly after the staging of *The Bus Stop,* which wore both modernism and alienation on its sleeve. Meanwhile, 1983 also saw the Ministry of Culture formulating a set of guidelines to regulate and ensure the "ideological correctness" of theatrical performances, including a stipulation that all programs first be examined and approved by a "sponsor unit" of cultural departments.[47] With anxieties about cultural pollution and contamination running high, there were any number of ways that a work of such hybridity as *The Bus Stop* could give offense. Against these shifting political currents, artist-intellectuals with modernist leanings took recourse in what may strike us as a strangely contradictory rhetoric—contradictory because decidedly "unmodernist" in the Western sense—namely, that of universal humanism.

More Than Jargon: The Rhetoric of Authenticity and One Humanity

I can tell you now that one of my main motives in coming here is to try to show that there is only one humanity. That our cultures and languages set up confusing sets of signals and these prevent us from communicating and sharing one another's thoughts and sensations, but that at the deeper levels where this play lives we are joined in a unity that is perhaps biological. (Arthur Miller, to the company of Chinese actors on their first meeting)[48]

I theorize a universality of human emotions; I hope that the production here of this very American play will simply assert the idea of a single humanity once again. (Arthur Miller, in a Beijing press conference)[49]

There is a convergence between the great geographical scope of the empires . . . and the empires . . . and the universalizing cultural discourses. Power makes this convergence possible, of course; with it goes the ability to be in far-flung places, to learn about other people, to codify and disseminate knowledge, to characterize, transport, install, and display instances of other cultures . . . and above all to rule them. (Edward Said)[50]

[Western] modernism took as its point of departure the questioning of the old Western humanism. In contrast, "this [our] modernism" rediscovers the once forfeited humanism under the specific conditions of Chinese social reality. (Gao Xingjian)[51]

The idea of humanism evacuates from itself all individual contradictions. It attempts to extricate itself from worldly contingencies that may yoke it to specific historical contexts, so that, at its limit, it inclines toward a universal and transcendent condition where all social horizons disappear.

In the West, it is an old and familiar idea, extending nostalgically back to Renaissance ideals of individual human dignity and potential. Within this tradition Miller makes his invocations of "one humanity," though it may be unsettling to hear him lay claims to knowledge of a "universal" humanity, knowledge to which the Chinese people are always somehow in want of direct and unmediated access. For when Miller asserts that "by some unplanned magic [they] may end up creating something not quite American *or* Chinese but a pure style springing from the heart of the play itself—the play as a nonnational event, that is, a human circumstance,"[52] it matters a great deal to Miller that it is not merely any artwork but *his* art and *his* plays that act as vessels of cultural transcendence. The lack of imperialist designs notwithstanding, this continual manifestation of an ethnocentric (not to say egocentric) attitude encourages and sustains such critical extrapolations as Said's—to wit, that the "convergence between the great geographical scope of the empires" and certain "universalizing cultural discourses" emanates from an imperializing power. On these terms, Miller plainly speaks as a cultural inheritor of this genealogy of power.

In post-Mao settings, on the other hand, the idea of humanism came to be writ even larger, though with quite different emphasis and orientation, by Chinese intellectuals. As Gao insightfully observes in this regard, Western modernism took as its point of departure the rediscovery of a "forfeited humanism." Gao has repeatedly lamented that, from the May Fourth period onward, Chinese intellectuals had sacrificed their rights as individuals and their autonomy as artists by pledging themselves to national politics.[53] The present entrance into modernity entailed more than just the import of foreign modernism: It involved crucially the reclamation, under the sign of "individuality," of things heretofore politicized for collective national objectives. Ironically, the most singular unit of "the individual," insofar as it was now made to stand for a politically neutral figure, thereby also became the most universal unit, because it was socially and ideologically unbounded. Into this sign of "the universal" were read those attributes of "human feelings" and "aesthetic vision," clichés certainly, but here tactically mobilized in the interests of recovering and justifying artistic autonomy and expressive freedom.

Several instances will serve to illustrate this point. In the early 1980s, in opposition to the prescriptive Socialist realism of Cultural Revolution days, there emerged a literature of critical reflection that attempted to revive a pre-Mao humanist perspective, whereby matters of love, morality, and other human emotions could be reconfigured as basic elements of human existence, separate and autonomous from politics.[54] At the same time, the advocates of literary modernism also cast their manifestos in the rhetoric of human emotions. In addition to Gao's modernist primer, *Preliminary Explorations in the Art and Technique of Modern Fiction,* 1981 also saw the publication of Sun Shaozhen's article, "A New Aesthetic Principle

Is Emerging." Though Sun never mentions Western modernism per se, his essay addresses the then-heated controversies surrounding *menglong* poetry and its appropriations of Western modernist poetics; in this vein, Sun defends the expression of human feelings, in whatever aesthetic form and of whatever cultural lineage, as a fundamental condition of artistic freedom. Finally, in a third related circumstance, directors of the 1980 Beijing production of *Macbeth,* aware of the play's signifying power as an allegory of the Maoist regime, took refuge in the rhetoric of artistic purity and authenticity in order to circumvent ever-imminent censure. While acknowledging the historical resemblance, they insisted that, first, the play was produced with meticulous fidelity to Shakespeare's "authorial inten-tion," and second, the enterprise was strictly an exploration in dramatic style and hence carried no ideological weight.[55] In all these instances, the common appeal to a discourse of human feelings and pure aesthetics worked to generate a category of the universal under which potentially risky articulations could be made independent of political currents.

While not diminishing genuine intellectual investments in the idea of humanism, it is nevertheless apparent that this combined rhetoric of uni-versality, aesthetic authenticity, and human emotions could not be extri-cated, despite transcendent inclinations, from its culturally specific effects as a "strategy of evasion." Helmut Martin has provided this illuminating term to denote the ways in which PRC intellectuals "conceived strategies that take them onto more remote levels of discourse, thereby avoiding head-on collisions with the policy-making level."[56] While Martin identi-fies the "foreign theme" as one strategy of evasion, by which writers used foreign settings or otherwise employed foreign literature as camouflage and "decoy" for expressing social criticism,[57] the complicated ideological web in which Western imports were always entangled made them more problematically negotiable. Indeed, this very business of negotiation was itself in need of evasive strategies that could neutralize the threat or accu-sation of "spiritual pollution." These two tasks were mutually reliant and supportive: on the one hand, the claim that appropriations and produc-tions of Western literature served purely aesthetic interests reinforced the claim that artistic practices constituted an autonomous sphere, indepen-dent of politics; and the assertion that there existed universal, ideologically neutral subjects rendered more tolerable the import and use of Western works upon exactly that premise. If the idea of universals had once been an apriority in Western history, in post-Mao China it was a tactical, and not easily granted, term. Indeed, its centrality in intellectual debates has led to the extravagant claim that anyone who discusses "universal values" both "rationally" and "in a publicly accessible form," no matter with what degree of conviction or denial, can essentially be classified as an "intellectual" in the distinct Chinese sense of *zhishi fenzi*.[58]

With reference to the theater, it is therefore fully explicable why Shakespearean productions received such attention during this period: Not only was Shakespeare the paragon of the pure and universal artist, but his advantageous location in a remote historical past effectively immunized him from any imputation of modernist decadence. Likewise, Miller represented a "safe" figure precisely because of his relatively realist dramatic style, and one sure symptom of *Salesman*'s ideological safety was, to put it bluntly, its nondenunciation and subsequent success. As the contexts now make clear, *Salesman* was perceived as valuable because it mediated not access into a universal human vision, but between classical realism and modernist experimentalism, a divide rife, as we have seen, with all kinds of political dangers and ramifications. Chinese artist-intellectuals invited Miller to direct his play not because they themselves could not comprehend its formal complexities or mount it without "outside help," but as yet another strategic maneuver through precarious social terrains. And what better proof of their faithfulness to "authorial intention" and "artistic authenticity" than having the playwright present as director and overseer?

By way of conclusion, we may take heed of the manner in which this cross-cultural episode testifies less to *Salesman*'s universality and transcendence, or its immanent translatability, than to the portability of culture in general: the transfer of a play from one national stage to another. Benjamin would add here that the signifying power of Miller's play, having perhaps been long exhausted, now received its proper reanimation and afterlife in post-Mao China. Entering into a country with its own developed discursive economy, both Miller's play and his personal rhetoric accrued resonance unforeseeable—and in this case, unseen—by the author himself even as he traveled in person to supervise every detail of the production. To the fact that his rhetoric of "single humanity" and "poetic vision" was absorbed into the host language of resistance and autonomy, and that his work and presence were deployed in the service of a local cultural-political project, Miller was peculiarly unalert. Indeed, it is more than a little ironic that this project seemed vitally contingent on Miller's ignorance on the ideological minefield over which he traversed. For only thus could artist-intellectuals posit their claims—not always made in good faith, thankfully—of the priority of the aesthetic, of the nonsubversive intention of their endeavors, and of the possibility of some degree of expressive (critical) freedom.

NOTES

1. Christopher Wren, "Willy Loman Gets China Territory," *New York Times,* May 7, 1983, 13.

2. Arthur Miller, *Salesman in Beijing* (New York:Viking, 1984), 229.

3. Jonathan Broder, "Arthur Miller and *Salesman* Hit the Road to Peking," *Chicago Tribune,* April 20, 1983, 1–2.

4. Miller, *Salesman in Beijing,* 49.

5. Edward W. Said, *Orientalism* (New York:Vintage, 1979).

6. According to Bette Bao Lord upon her visit to China in 1984, *Salesman* was enjoying a run second only to the classic Chinese drama *Teahouse.* From "*Salesman* in Beijing," *New York,* May 14, 1984, 77–78.

7. In a press conference in Beijing later that year, Miller recalled: "I was invited to Beijing to direct an all-Chinese version of *Death of a Salesman* by Cao Yu, the famous playwright and chairman of the Chinese Theater Association. The invitation was a shock at first. I don't speak Chinese, there was a whole illusion that we are so far apart culturally that it would take me forever to make things relatively comprehensible to actors. . . . All these problems came up, but I think I was too frightened. Literally I was speaking English and they were speaking Chinese, but underneath we really had a common language." From "Arthur Miller on Directing His Own Play in China," *China Reconstructs* 32, no. 8 (August 1983): 9–10.

8. Brenda Murphy, *Miller: Death of a Salesman* (Cambridge: Cambridge University Press, 1995).

9. Murphy, *Miller,* 121–23.

10. Edward W. Said, *Beginnings: Intention and Method* (New York: Basic Books, 1975), 5.

11. Miller, *Salesman in Beijing,* vii.

12. Miller, *Salesman in Beijing,* 1.

13. John Woodruff, *China in Search of Its Future: Reform vs. Repression, 1982–1989* (New York: Carol Publishing, 1990), 89–90.

14. See Bill Brugger and Stephen Reglar, *Politics, Economy, and Society in Contemporary China* (Stanford, CA: Stanford University Press, 1994), 229.

15. See Constantine Tung, "Introduction: Tradition and Experience of the Drama of the People's Republic of China," in *Drama in the People's Republic of China,* ed. Constantine Tung and Colin Mackerras (New York: State University of New York Press, 1987), 1–27.

16. Tung, "Introduction," in Tung and Mackerras, *Drama,* 3.

17. See Shiao-Ling S. Yu, "Introduction," *Chinese Drama after the Cultural Revolution, 1979–1989: An Anthology,* ed. Shiao-Ling S.Yu (New York: Edwin Mellen Press, 1996), 2.

18. Quoted in Tung, "Introduction," in Tung and Mackerras, *Drama,* 5; originally in *Renmin Ribao,* June 11, 1972, 4.

19. Quoted in Mabel Lee, "Walking Out of Other People's Prisons: Liu Zaifu and Gao Xingjian on Chinese Literature in the 1990s," *Asian and African Studies* 5 (1996): 98–102; originally in "Bali suibi" ("Jottings from Paris"), *Guangchang zazhi* 4, no. 32 (1991): 15.

20. See Brugger and Reglar, "Intellectuals and Struggles" in *Politics, Economy, and Society*, 225–60.

21. See Tung, "Introduction," in Tung and Mackerras, *Drama,* 9–11.

22. See Yan Haiping, "Theater and Society: An Introduction to Contemporary Chinese Drama," in *Theater and Society: An Anthology of Contemporary Chinese Drama,* ed. Yan Haiping (Armonk, NY: M.E. Sharpe, 1998), ix–xlvi.

23. See Brugger and Reglar, *Politics, Economy, and Society,* 250–51.

24. Miller, *Salesman in Beijing, 233.*

25. Xiaomei Chen, *Occidentalism: A Theory of Counter-Discourse in Post-Mao China* (New York: Oxford University Press, 1995), 133; originally in *Renmin xiju* 2 (1982): 40–44.

26. For a brief overview of various forms of fictional writing in this period, see Peter Li, "Social Malaise as Reflected in the Literature of the 1980s," in *Culture and Politics in China: An Anatomy of Tiananmen Square,* ed. Peter Li, Steven Mark, and Marjorie H. Li (New Brunswick, NJ: Transaction, 1991), 225–42. For a discussion of the controversy surrounding *menglong* poetry, see Chen's chapter "'Misunderstanding' Western Modernism: The *Menglong* Movement," in *Occidentalism,* 69–98.

27. Lee, "Walking Out of Other People's Prisons," 98.

28. Xiaobing Tang, "The Function of New Theory: What Does It Mean to Talk about Postmodernism in China?" in *Politics, Ideology and Literary Discourse in Modern China: Theoretical Interventions and Cultural Critique,* ed. Liu Kang and Xiaobing Tang (Durham, NC: Duke University Press, 1993), 278–99.

29. See William Tay, "Avant-garde Theater in Post-Mao China: *The Bus Stop* by Gao Xingjian," in *Worlds Apart: Recent Chinese Writing and Its Audiences,* ed. Howard Goldblatt (Armonk, NY: M. E. Sharpe, 1990), 111–18; originally in *Wenyi bao* 8 (1984): 14–19.

30. Gao Xingjian, *The Bus Stop,* in *Chinese Drama after the Cultural Revolution, 1979–1989: An Anthology,* ed. Shiao-Ling S. Yu (New York: Edwin Mellen Press, 1996), 233–89.

31. See for reference Yu, "Introduction," in *Chinese Drama,* 17; Woodruff, *China,* 29; and Tay, "Avant-garde Theater," in Goldblatt, *Worlds Apart,* 112–15. For a fuller critical comparison of the two plays, see Kwok-Kan Tam, "Drama of Dilemma: Waiting as Form and Motif in *The Bus Stop* and *Waiting for Godot,*" in *Studies in Chinese-Western Comparative Drama,* ed. Yun-Tong Luk (Hong Kong: Chinese University Press, 1990), 23–45.

32. See "Author's Suggestions for the Performance of *The Bus Stop,*" appended to Gao, *The Bus Stop,* in Yu, *Chinese Drama,* 286–87.

33. Gao, *The Bus Stop,* in Yu, *Chinese Drama,* 265.

34. For a catalogue of plays produced in each year, see relevant volumes of *China: Facts and Figures Annual.*

35. See Chen, *Occidentalism,* 64–65.

36. He Wen, "On Seeing the Play *The Bus Stop,*" trans. Chan Sin-wai, *Renditions* 19/20 (1983): 387–92. According to Tay, this double issue of *Renditions* was not published until the end of 1984, while the Chinese version first appeared in *Wenyi bao* 3 (1984): 21–25.

37. Quoted in Tay, "Avant-garde Theater," in Goldblatt, *Worlds Apart,* 115.

38. He, "On Seeing the Play *The Bus Stop,*" 390.

39. Chen, *Occidentalism,* 51.

40. Jing Wang, *High Culture Fever: Politics, Aesthetics, and Ideology in Deng's China* (Berkeley: University of California Press, 1996), 169; originally in *Wenxue piping* 3 (1988): 13.

41. Lee, "Walking Out of Other People's Prisons," 100.

42. He, "On Seeing the Play *The Bus Stop,*" 392.

43. Quoted in Lee, "Walking Out of Other People's Prisons," 103.

44. Wang, *High Culture Fever,* 169.

45. Gao, *The Bus Stop,* in Yu, *Chinese Drama,* 266.

46. For details on this campaign, see Brugger and Reglar, *Politics, Economy, and Society,* 253–55.

47. See John L. Scherer, ed., *China: Facts and Figures Annual,* Vol. 7 (Gulf Breeze, FL: Academic International Press, 1984), 236.

48. Miller, *Salesman in Beijing,* 5.

49. Miller, *Salesman in Beijing,* 44.

50. Edward W. Said, *Culture and Imperialism* (New York: Vintage, 1994), 108.

51. Quoted in Wang, *High Culture Fever,* 170.

52. Miller, *Salesman in Beijing,* 155.

53. See the discussion of Gao's "The Myth of the Nation and Insanity for the Individual," in Lee, "Walking Out of Other People's Prisons," 107–8.

54. See Li, "Social Malaise," in Li, Mark, and Li, *Culture and Politics in China,* 230–31.

55. Discussed in Chen, *Occidentalism,* 53.

56. Helmut Martin, "The Drama *Tragic Song of Our Time (Shidai de beige):* Functions of Literature in the Eighties and Its Socio-Political Limitations," in Tung and MacKerras, *Drama,* 254–81.

57. Martin, "The Drama *Tragic Song of Our Time,*" in Tung and Mackerras, *Drama,* 263–65.

58. Brugger and Reglar, *Politics, Economy, and Society,* 225–26.

Mariagabriella Cambiaghi

Directing Miller in Italy

Arthur Miller's stage history in Italy coincides with two notable events: the widening of national repertoires to include contemporary foreign dramaturgy and the opportunity for a modern way of staging plays in a revitalized theater. After twenty years of fascist dictatorship, which meant the banishment of contemporary foreign works from Italian theaters and the ascendance of repertoires based on light comedy and a few classics, the aftermath of the Second World War marked the discovery of contemporary foreign, in particular French and American, dramaturgy. To Italian audiences this new momentum had an extraordinarily innovative power: deeply realistic texts, which were often socially relevant, could be performed and less than heroic characters might be displayed in highly charged atmospheres. This broadening of theatrical and cultural horizons found its first interpreters in a generation of directors who were to lay the foundations of contemporary Italian theater, in particular Luigi Squarzina and Luchino Visconti.

As early as 1947, Squarzina staged the new American play *All My Sons,* directing the highly regarded Maltagliati-Gassman company in a cast that included Evi Maltagliati and a young talent, Vittorio Gassman. The play, first performed at Teatro Quirino in Rome on November 4, 1947, bewildered an Italian audience, one that had been used to receiving a play's reassuring platitudes. Miller's work introduced a portrait of America far from the cliché of happy endings familiar from popular Hollywood movies. In addition, the text impressed critics because of the topical interest of its subject and the strict accuracy of language employed by the young and provocative American playwright.

However, it was Luchino Visconti who was responsible for Miller's first success in postwar Italy. Visconti revealed, in his production of *Death of a Salesman,* the contradictions in the long-celebrated American dream. Performed in Rome exactly two years after its American premiere, the play opened at the Teatro Eliseo on February 10, 1951, and was triumphally welcomed by both the audience and major critics. Reviewers underlined the careful correspondence between text and staging; such a result was achieved by an extremely innovative use of lighting that split the stage into multiple performance spaces. Gianni Polidori's design followed Miller's stage directions, introducing a fixed scene that represented a section of the Loman house as well as its rooms. The background featured reproductions of skyscrapers that insinuated their presence through the open roof of the house, generating a feeling of oppression, as if the house and its inhabitants were constantly in danger of being crushed.

The stylistic accuracy of design was mirrored in the way Visconti chose to stress the tragic quality of the play. Paolo Stoppa as Willy and Rina Morelli as Linda uncovered the complexity and intensity of Miller's dramatic composition. Visconti worked with his actors to search for the intricate and perplexing "interior realism" that could be found in the dramatic text. Commenting on his experience with *Death of a Salesman,* Visconti pointed out how fundamental this text had been to his work as a director:

> Directing *Death of a Salesman* was an important experience to me. . . . it hardly ever happens—along a difficult and adventurous path such as contemporary theater is—to find true and authentic texts such as Miller's: there you come across everyday life, you hear words people speak everyday in their homes, in the street, everywhere. In Miller's plays we feel the dramatic sense of American life, the suffocating presence of machines in human existence, exactly because of that extremely detailed fabric of actual facts. This terrible reality speaks by itself: it is enough to detail [it] in all its intensity. That is what I have been trying to do.[1]

It should come as no surprise, then, that the Italian director would return on several occasions to plays written by the American author with whom he shared similar ideological and artistic values. As early as 1955, Visconti staged *The Crucible* and showed how a tragedy centered on an ugly episode in American history could also be relevant to Italy by universally symbolizing the violence of power and intolerance.[2] The play had already been performed in a French version in 1954 in Venice, directed by Guy Reguier under the title *La Chasse aux sorcières.* Visconti's production made clear just how different this play was from *Death of a*

Salesman: "The private drama has become a public one, whereas a little common tragedy has become each man's tragedy, whenever he has to face his own responsibility either civil or collective."[3] Visconti collaborated on the translation into Italian,[4] taking into consideration the double perspective of the plot: the actual history supported by the records of the Salem trials and the human tragedy affecting the individuals, who are recreated in Miller's play. Visconti centered the dramatic conflict on the psychological core of the characters in order to shed light on the hysteria that dominates the small community, the self-righteousness of accusers, the cruel logic of inquisitors, and the spiritual anguish of victims. He emphasized passion and the strong force of fierce emotion in constant excitement; he urged his actors to "overact," even to shout their lines. In this way general events cast their ominous shadow on individuals; episodes grew larger and affected people's reactions beyond measure, as the performance's mounting emphasis on action and sharp tones clearly showed how history and private matters merged in a balance far from any normal reality.

Visual aspects played an important role in their impact on the audience. The director conceived an imposing setting that was influenced by his work on opera productions in previous years. The costumes were inspired by Flemish seventeenth-century painting and had great suggestive power, displaying a sculptural quality and a meticulousness in reproduction. All of the design elements reinforced the production's emotional strength without compromising the imposing themes in the text. But Visconti's mise-en-scène proved to be the occasion for a critical debate that consisted of two main aspects: the artistic value of the play, whose high social significance was unanimously appreciated, and the effectiveness of Visconti's direction.

Some critics refused to recognize in the play any considerable poetic worth, as they saw it as didactic and self-evident; at the same time, the playwright's analysis of the psychological mechanisms that underlie modern fanaticism was criticized for not going far enough. Some reviewers were disappointed by the melodramatic style of both sumptuous scenery and unrestrained acting; these choices seemed to diffuse the play's potent political content. On the other hand, both the playwright and director received complete approval from progressive critics, who appreciated the play's ideological and artistic worth.[5]

In January 1958 Visconti staged *A View from the Bridge,* another Italian premiere of Miller, but this one a cruel and violent tragedy centered on a true story set among Italian emigrants. Visconti was fascinated by the dark events narrated in the play and by the clash between the primeval instinct of individuals and common morality. He started, as usual, with a careful study of the text and concluded that an Italian interpretation of the play would not sound correct unless Marco and Rodolpho speak with a strong Sicilian accent. Thus, Visconti chose to translate the English lines of the two characters with words and phrases taken from Sicilian dialect.[6] As the director explained to the playwright:

> From an Italian point of view there exists, in *A View from the Bridge,* a linguistic problem a director cannot possibly ignore. All our best films show traces of the opportunity of realism which is inherent in dialects. . . . We consider the things you recount in your play as an integral part of our national experience and we have been doing our best to represent it—as a tragedy of our own flesh and blood—and we have been giving it the same respect, the same devotion, compassion and understanding you so fully showed to your characters.[7]

As usual, Visconti's staging adopted a powerful and suggestive design, and he made use of cinematographic techniques that he had already tested in his film production: in a theatrical adaptation of a tracking shot, audience members were transported from a general view of New York to Eddie Carbone's house, to its interior, and, through a well-timed play of lights, to a close-up of the protagonist. These effects were obtained by a disciplined use of lighting and of colored tulle that systematically unveiled new elements of the design. In the last scene the imposing shape of the Brooklyn Bridge, the profile of skyscrapers, and the neighborhood crowds gathered on fire escapes—where the washing had been hung out to dry—stood out against the light in the background while, on the proscenium, the protagonists silently realized that a catastrophe had just occurred.

The relationship between Visconti and Miller ended with a production staged abroad: *After the Fall (Après la chute)* was performed at the Théâtre du Gymnase in Paris on January 19, 1965.[8] Critics rejected the show and turned against Miller's text, which they described as simultaneously overly intellectual and superficial. Visconti's spectacular staging was also criticized. Focusing on choral and social elements of the play, he had chosen to make the relationship between the two protagonists fade into the background in order to show how the characters were indeed tormented by postwar, collective American obsessions. The scenery furthered this interpretation by recalling the threat of the twentieth-century European nightmare of annihilation and genocide. By means of a transparent backcloth and an opportune play of lights, the action was matched—or better, dominated—by the alternating outlines of skyscrapers and Auschwitz's ominous watchtower (also present in Miller's stage directions). At the same time, the broad style of acting sensationalized the message of denunciation ascribed to the play. Italian critics were more generous than their French colleagues in acknowledging, at the very least, the ambitious drive Visconti had shown in his original mise-en-scène, which tried to point out collective responsibilities, even at the risk of offending some members of his French audience.

Visconti set in motion the Italian tradition of interpreting Miller's work for the stage. But two other major directors were also responsible for the premiere productions of his plays in their Italian translations. Giorgio Strehler's version of *A Memory of Two Mondays* was produced at the Piccolo Teatro in Milan in 1962. The Italian maestro avoided Miller's most celebrated plays, which would have led to a comparison with Visconti, and worked on this one-act play instead. The play, in Strehler's view so reminiscent of Anton Chekhov, was presented on a double bill with Bertolt Brecht's *The Exception to the Rule*. It marked the only encounter between Strehler and Miller, whose major themes and dramatic style were not really central to the director's interests.

Much more remarkable was the Italian premiere of *After the Fall* in Rome on October 21, 1964. Franco Zeffirelli, formerly Visconti's designer, directed the play. He worked with two prominent actors and decided to concentrate especially on their two roles, focusing on the conflict between Quentin, portrayed by a young Giorgio Albertazzi, and Maggie, played by the film actress Monica Vitti. What Zeffirelli tried to do was to clarify the protagonist's obscure existential torment, which goes beyond Miller's autobiographical allusions (although the references to Marilyn Monroe attracted a large audience in Italy, too). The scenery, as conceived by the director himself, supported this basic critical interpretation of a more fundamental human anxiety: a metal trestle enclosed the stage as a geometric and oppressive frame. What critics saw was a sincere homage paid to the text and to its author by the director and actors, as their famous production transformed what might have seemed cold and intellectual into a performance full of emotional resonance.[9]

One of the peculiarities of Italian theater, at least until the 1950s, was that actors served as managers and inspirers of stage productions; Miller's dramatic compositions attracted their interest not only because of the situations they represented, but even more so because of their rich and fascinating characters. Since the end of the 1960s, it has been actors who have largely supported Miller's works on the Italian stage, and they have used his characters as vehicles through which to display their own craft. Raf Vallone, who was the leading man in Peter Brook's 1958 *A View from the Bridge* in Paris and in Sidney Lumet's film version in 1962, played Eddie again in an Italian production he also directed in 1967. His performance was a personal triumph, although the production was not particularly innovative. Vallone's affection for the American playwright was deeply rooted: he directed the premiere of *The Price* in 1969, in which he acted with Mario Scaccia, and he later staged a second version of the same play in 1987.

Among Miller's characters, however, Willy Loman has certainly been the most attractive role for Italian actors to perform, and consequently *Death of a Salesman* has been the most frequently staged Miller play in Italy. Once its politically and socially subversive drive had lost some of its initial force, the play was still popular on the stage precisely because of the strength of its characters, overwhelmed by unfulfillable dreams and betrayed by the world's false values. To a modern Italian sensibility, Willy is no longer only a victim of capitalism; rather, he seems the prey of his own deceptive dreams and of his will to transform his sons' as well as his own worthlessness into the stature of a myth.

Several Italian actors have taken their measure against this modern antihero. Among the most important ones are: Tino Buazzelli in 1975 (directed by Edmo Fenoglio), Carlo Hintermann in 1982 (directed by Orazio Costa), Giulio Borsetti in 1986 (directed by Marco Sciaccaluga), and Enrico Maria Salerno in 1992 (directed by Franco Zeffirelli). All of these interpretations were warmly received by both enthusiastic audiences and critics. As a matter of fact, Miller's plays have become in the course of time a longed-for test for many actors, but since Visconti's work they generally have had no part in the projects of the great Italian directors. Faithful but not very original mise-en-scènes have been the norm in productions emphasizing the protagonist's role.

Even Mario Missiroli, who avoids banality and marks his productions with an original and coherent style, has had a problematic history in staging Miller. Missiroli directed a production of *All My Sons* in 1989 and the Italian premiere of *Broken Glass* in 1995. For *All My Sons* he created a fixed and surreal design offering a double perspective on the interior and exterior of a Georgian house, which eventually became the site where characters revealed their highly personal dramas. Under Missiroli's direction, Joe Keller, played by Gastone Moschin, lost much of his historical relevance and became a neurotic man, tormented by sins committed in a past he could not forget.

Missiroli directed the famous Italian actress Valeria Moriconi, founder of the Teatro Stabile delle Marche, in the role of Sylvia in *Broken Glass*, which opened in Bologna at the Arena del Sole. He transformed the text into a series of snapshots to be displayed before the audience's eyes. The designer, Enrico Job, enhanced this effect by using a revolving stage to control the movement of the dark furniture decorating the scene, while pictures of New York were projected onto a backcloth. Actors were given great independence in interpretation, even though the creative process was guided by the director according to his general stylistic sense of the show. Critics were especially taken by the bravura performances of the actors: Valeria Moriconi's mournful and passionate portrait of wife and woman—"a Cassandra foreseeing Nazi folly," as the actress described her role[10]—was filled with references to theatrical make-believe.

An interesting attempt to reinterpret the mise-en-scènes of Miller's plays was made by Giancarlo Cobelli, one of the most unconventional and iconoclastic directors in Italy, famous for his rereadings of the classical repertory. In 1997, Cobelli was asked by the Teatro Eliseo in Rome and by Umberto Orsini, who wished to play the role of Willy Loman, to stage a new production of *Death of a Salesman*. Cobelli began by cutting any element in the script that might sound obsolete. He resolved to limit the social and political components as much as possible; thus, he eliminated all close references to postwar America in order to concentrate on the psychological aspects of the protagonists. The production focused on "the calvary of a negative hero" by means of an expressionist rhythm in which reality was split into flickering memories; action, as the director said, "became epic" and narrated the protagonist's mental processes in a series of stops uniting past and present.[11]

Such an interpretation required the design to be far from naturalistic. Paolo Tommasi's set used a linear black-and-white wall to divide the stage into two sections; and the interior of Willy's house disappeared, as did any recognizable room in it. Some doors (presumably those of the rooms) were displayed on the wall by a play of lights, while the action took place either on the proscenium, when set in the present, or behind the wall, which became transparent whenever past memories were involved. Spare, unadorned pieces of furniture—coffee tables, chairs, a bed, some boxes—completed the scenery and were ready to slide into the wings when necessary, while on the backcloth black-and-white silhouettes of trees and small houses, devoured by uncontrolled urbanization, were floodlit every now and then. Tommasi's costume designs discreetly removed any realistic reference to America; in fact, they emphasized the proletarian origin of the protagonists, who turned out to be in this interpretation "country people overwhelmed by the reality of a big town."[12] The sharp figurative stylization was also captured in the music composed by Antonio Lucifero. Starting with a crash of thunder announcing the protagonist's first appearance on stage carrying two huge suitcases, the musical motif consisted of amplified sounds both natural and artificial, supporting either the beginning or the end of Willy's flashbacks, as though beating out the rhythm of his hallucinations. Yet as most critics pointed out, such choices, even though they were supported by a rigorous faithfulness to Miller's text, eventually undermined the essence of the play. What critics registered as flaws were the show's constant striving for equilibrium between realism and symbolism and its persistent attention to expressionist atmospheres, all played upon rigid contrasts between black and white.[13] The acting was nevertheless very convincing, mainly because of the presence of two actors at the height of their expressive maturity, Umberto Orsini and Giulia Lazzarini.

Although critics did not uniformly praise Cobelli's *Death of a Salesman,* his production was greatly appreciated by audiences and might be looked upon as a sort of model for new stagings of Miller's plays. Miller offers the Italian theater a series of disciplined dramatic structures; the only risk is misrepresentation, but for the future of Miller in Italy, it is a risk worth taking.

Translated by Lisanna Calvi and Enoch Brater

NOTES

1. Luchino Visconti, "Nota sulla *Morta di un commesso viaggiatore* e sul *Crogiuolo,*" *Il Contemporaneo,* May 22, 1954.

2. The Italian premiere of *The Crucible,* directed and designed by Visconti, took place in Rome on November 15, 1955, at the Teatro Quirino.

3. Visconti, "Nota sulla *Morta di un commesso viaggiatore* e sul *Crogiuolo.*"

4. The Italian translation of *The Crucible* by Visconti and Gino Bardi was later published in the series *Teatro Einaudi* (Torino: Einaudi, 1959).

5. See, for example, Nicola Chiaromonte, "le streghe di Visconti," *Il Mondo,* November 29, 1955.

6. Sebastiano Lo Monaco was the first Sicilian actor to play Eddie Carbone; he did so in a production for Teatro di Messina staged by Giuseppe Paroni Griffi in the 2003–4 season. See Enoch Brater, *Arthur Miller: A Playwright's Life and Works* (London: Thames and Hudson, 2005), 79.

7. Luchino Visconti, *Lettera ad Arthur Miller,* dated January 8, 1958; published in *Il Contemporaneo,* January 18, 1958.

8. This production, designed by Mario Garbuglia with costumes by Christian Dior, used a French translation by Henri Robillot. On the design elements of this interpretation, see Garbuglia's comments in Bruno Villen, *Luchino Visconti* (Milano: Garzanti, 1978), 179.

9. For details of this production, see Matthew Roudané, ed., *Conversations with Arthur Miller* (Jackson: University of Mississippi Press, 1987), 103–4, 107; Janet N. Balakian, "The Holocaust, the Depression, and McCarthyism: Miller in the Sixties," in *The Cambridge Companion to Arthur Miller,* ed. Christopher Bigsby (Cambridge: Cambridge University Press, 1997), 121–22; and Brater, *Arthur Miller,* 99. In 1966 Marcello Mastroianni played the role of Quentin in the Zeffirelli production.

10. See Simonetta Rabiony, "Commandante Valeria," *La Stampa,* February 16, 1995.

11. See Giancarlo Cobelli, program notes, "Nota di regia," Teatro Eliseo, Rome, 1997.

12. Cobelli, program notes.

13. See, for example, Giovanni Raboni, "Miller, I sogni infanti di un commesso viaggiatore," *Corriere della Sera,* November 17, 1997.

Robert Gordon

Guilty Secrets and Cultural Blind Spots
Miller's Plays in South Africa

The history of modern South Africa is replete with ironies, more often grim than comic. Not surprisingly, the political complexities of the country's recent societal transformations have shaped the history of the production and reception of Arthur Miller's plays in much the same way as they have determined South African cultural life in general. To trace the progress of Miller's reputation in South Africa is to unravel a network of paradoxes that reveals how the actual interplay of British colonialism, American-style capitalism, and Calvinist fundamentalism in South African society finds a focus in the themes of Miller's major dramas, while the theater community itself treated the plays as modern classics rather than emphasizing their immediate relevance. The rare professional appearance of Miller's plays, from the first production in 1956 of *The Crucible* by Leonard Schach to the same director's staging of *The Price* in 1977, offered white South Africans an extremely potent image of their own collusion with an immoral system.[1]

For twenty years after the Second World War, English-language South African theater was still largely colonial.[2] From the midfifties, however, a postcolonial indigenous South African theater began to emerge under the auspices of the state-subsidized, English- and Afrikaans-language National Theatre, and a number of commercial managements led by such progressive figures as Leon Gluckman and Leonard Schach and the more populist Brian Brooke. Until the late eighties, commercial managements like Pieter Toerien continued to import British actors in prestigious South African productions; some of these actors were seduced by the combined attractions of sunshine and easy living and remained permanently in South Africa after their initial contracts had ended. It was only in the midseventies, with the emergence of Brian Astbury and Yvonne Bryceland's Space Theatre in Cape Town and the Market Theatre in Johannesburg, that indigenous South African theater can be said to have come of age.

Between 1958 and 1975, Athol Fugard was one of the few white theater practitioners to attempt to work with black theater artists on equal
terms. With the notable exception of a handful of black playwrights
such as Herbert Dhlomo in the thirties and forties, the populist Gibson
Kente in the sixties and seventies, and Zakes Mda together with a few
black consciousness practitioners in the seventies, professional black theater was barely visible until the early eighties. When in the late seventies
indigenous South African theater did begin to manifest itself, it was ruth-
lessly censored and survived through the strategy of presenting clandes-
tine performances that aimed to further the struggle. This new theater
was committed to the destruction of apartheid and the overthrow of the
Afrikaner-dominated regime. In the context of the antiapartheid battle,
there was little room for theater that was not highly politicized and relevant to the immediate political situation.

The art theater was dominated by conservative humanists and
white liberals who, constrained by a ruthless system of censorship,
cautiously championed the work of black writers and performers at
the Market Theatre, Johannesburg, and the Space Theatre, Cape Town.
During the period of the cultural boycott of South Africa (midsixties
to the early nineties), white South Africans retreated even deeper into
their cultural laager, and—with three notable exceptions—Miller's
plays were chiefly performed in amateur productions by university
theater departments and other tertiary educational establishments.[3] In
the absence of a serious professional repertoire of world drama, these
productions were often accorded art theater status by journalists and
critics.

The early history of South African productions of Miller's work
is inextricably bound up with what might be described as the British
colonial mentality. The first professional production of a Miller play was
Schach's production of *The Crucible* at the Labia Theatre, Cape Town, in
1956. Few records of this production have survived, but the cast included
two pioneering Afrikaans actors, Andre Huguenet, as Danforth, and
Johann Nell, as Reverend Hale, with Proctor played by the well-known
British actor, Joss Ackland, then at the beginning of his distinguished
career. Schach was a cultured man who made a habit of staging productions of the prestigious drama that he had seen in London and
New York, and it is likely that the production was heavily influenced
by the British premiere that year. Schach did another production of
The Crucible for the Witwatersrand University Players, Johannesburg, in
1959, with a cast of amateur actors that included Molly Seftel, who later

became associated with the work of Athol Fugard and other progressive theater makers.

The Johannesburg Repertory Players' production of *A View from the Bridge,* in 1958, was directed by Schach, who modeled his production on the London premiere of the two-act version. The interpretation of the play offered seems typical of the fairly conservative and colonial attitude of the late fifties in South Africa. It is seen in humanist terms as a universal tragedy, transcending local historical and political differences. Miller's own formulation of the tragedy of the common man is repeated without acknowledgment of its source, as proof of the high cultural status of the performance. The production toured Cape Town and Durban, where the mayor made a speech of thanks at the opening night, another sign of the status of such an art event within the civic calendar of a colonial city.

The note of self-congratulation reflects the colonials' sense of inferiority in a particular manner. Although New York is mentioned, there is no sense that the production in any way attempted to express the specific identity of the Italian immigrant community of Brooklyn. The drama is regarded as a modern species of ancient Greek tragedy while the production is modeled on the performance the director saw in London, "where it was privately performed having been banned for public performance."[4] The assertion that Schach's production follows a classical pattern emphasizes the high cultural pedigree, drawing attention away from the fact that the play's London banning was a response both to its presentation of a repressed current of confused homosexual feeling (Eddie's crude kissing of Rodolpho is a clumsy attempt to mock him for his effeminacy) and to its portrayal of Eddie's incestuous desire for his niece.

The social analysis that is invariably one of the poles of Miller's psychosocial presentation of the American family is never directly alluded to. The universality of the tragic paradigm is assumed. Its genesis within a specific subculture as an aspect of a society whose economic inequalities Miller never ceased to castigate, apparently went unnoticed in South Africa in 1958. The production was blind to Miller's portrayal of the insecure identity of the immigrant male in the melting pot culture and to the psychosexual conflicts that are played out to their conclusion as a desperate betrayal of those Eddie loves. Eddie's self-destructive assertion of the primitive value of masculinity is more precisely explained with reference to his particular sense of social and cultural inferiority than to any generalized Sophoclean pattern of self-immolation. In what seems typical of the South African approach to performing Miller, the production emphasized the emotional intensity of the characters' conflicts while ignoring the writer's careful depiction of their sources in a specific stratum of American society.[5]

After South Africa declared itself a republic and was forced to leave the British Commonwealth in 1961, whites increasingly turned away from Britain and toward the United States to find valorizing images of success and power. The American dream became a South African dream, easily attainable by most whites. The combination of enormous natural resources, cheap labor, and a warm and sunny climate allowed the vast majority of white South Africans to enjoy a standard of living unattainable by any but the wealthiest Californians.

Such easy affluence rendered the logic of *Death of a Salesman* unfathomable and is one reason why the play may only have received one (semiprofessional) production, by David Bloomberg in Cape Town, before the high-profile production by the Performing Arts Council of the Transvaal (PACT), starring the well-known actor Joe Stewardson in 1975.[6] Although there were professional productions of *The Crucible* by PACT in 1975 (directed by Barney Simon) and in 1981 (directed by William Egan) as well as a large number of university productions, *Death of a Salesman* was not revived again until the much-praised production of 2001.[7] Neither the 1975 production nor the 2001 revival emphasized the capitalist myth of commercial success as the root cause of Willy's self-delusion, so neither of them was able to connect Miller's exposure of the human price of a capitalist system with the price South Africans were paying for exploiting American-style capitalism as a means of sustaining its inhumane system of racist fundamentalism.[8]

In an irony of the kind that seems to typify modern South African history, the Pretoria State Theatre production of *Death of a Salesman* that opened at the Grahamstown Arts Festival in July 2000 became something of a cause célèbre. Surprisingly, this highly praised production was not generally conceived by critics in postapartheid South Africa as in any sense a critique of the capitalist value system, but rather as a play about a small man's misguided sense of failure. In commending Bobby Heaney's production, reviewers both exploited the opportunity to castigate the Ministry of Culture for having withdrawn government funding from the State Theatre (under the auspices of the PACT, a former showplace of the apartheid government), while praising the enterprise of the company for becoming shareholders and continuing the planned tour of the production to Cape Town, Johannesburg, and Pretoria on a commercial basis. The political implications of this successful enterprise were viewed as consistent with the meaning of the play. Guy Willoughby interpreted the connection between the play and the circumstances of its production at the Baxter Theatre, Cape Town, in concluding his review:

> If Willy's tragedy is that he finally gives in to the forces that crush him, the play's radicalism subsists in precisely this: we need not give in to despair, but can choose hope and change. In South Africa today as we contemplate the crisis in the arts, there is much in this message to build on and applaud. Heaney and his cast—and dramatic art at its best—are triumphantly vindicated.[9]

This interpretation of the play seems to owe more to the white reviewer's desire to criticize Thabo Mbeki's African National Congress government for its populist "African Renaissance" rhetoric than to a close reading of the play's text. The government's decision to cut subsidies for what it perceived as Eurocentric high art led to a crisis among previously state-funded white theater professionals. In seeking to commend the enterprise of white theater practitioners for championing great art within a market-driven economy, the reviewer, paradoxically, wrests a capitalist message from Miller's play. It is quite clear in *Death of a Salesman* that Willy's deluded belief in commercial success is the wrong dream. It is misguided courage that leads him to commit suicide rather than to accept his average status as an ordinary human being. Linda does not represent "hope and change" when she laments Willy's suicide; she merely regrets the fact that he could not accept the compromise of surviving without grandiose dreams in an imperfect world.

Apparently unaware of the potential irony, one of the production's commercial backers explained the relevance of the play for the businessmen who came to its rescue:

> It just seemed so sad that this production was in danger because of the State Theatre's closure. I felt that I'd like to do my bit for the arts. I've seen the play before, and I know how brilliant it is. I just got excited at the thought of helping. We've bought out a whole performance for our staff and clients, and the response is wonderful. We're all salesmen, you know![10]

Most reviewers offered revisionist readings of the play that are entirely uncritical of Willy's blindness. Typical of such sentimental interpretations is Toni Muller's praise for Miller's "beautiful and tender story of a salesman who was looking for that one big sale, the one that would secure the family financially so that he could follow the real dream he never realized, that of carpentry and handiwork."[11] Christina Kennedy's glib summary of the play's themes is a further example of the reviewers' desire to recuperate the meaning of the play as an existentialist depiction of the human condition rather than a critique of capitalism:

> . . . the themes laid bare by Miller—although penned over 50 years ago—are as relevant today as they were back then. Corporate back-stabbing, infidelity, the ravages of stress and financial worries, father and son tensions, shattered hopes and dreams, societal claustrophobia . . . so what's changed? . . . Sad to say, being a nice guy doesn't necessarily lead to success and happiness. Maybe that's why the government has decided "no more Mr. Nice Guy" with the State Theatre.

The experience of an anti-Communist witch hunt in South Africa from the midfifties to the midsixties was even more traumatic than the McCarthy trials had been in the United States. Unashamed of employing violent means to destroy all effective political opposition to the state, the Nationalist government exploited the anti-Communist rhetoric of the cold war to justify ruthless suppression of any form of antiapartheid activism. The culmination of this witch hunt was the infamous Rivonia Trial that led to Nelson Mandela's thirty-year incarceration on Robben Island.[12] Despite the relative paucity of professional productions, *The Crucible* was clearly the one play of Miller's that most haunted liberal South Africans. A review of the 1997 film starring Daniel Day-Lewis and Paul Scofield noted that its "resoundingly local relevance will be lost on no one."[13] But that was five years after an ANC government had replaced the apartheid regime and dismantled its repressive police system. By the time the film was released, the Mandela government's Truth and Reconciliation Commission had offered the possibility that a public confrontation between victims of apartheid violence and their oppressors might lead to a healing process to reconcile past enemies. There was, however, a grave danger that the revision of recent history it produced would polarize opinion in such a way as to permit a rationalization of police brutality on the one hand, or to provoke a series of vigilante witch hunts against the apartheid oppressors on the other.

Miller's Salem has thus provided an image that illuminates two of the most traumatic moments in modern South African history. From the late fifties to the late eighties, *The Crucible* was the play that most perfectly encoded the secret guilt of white liberals who stood to profit materially from a system they opposed—a guilt that was energetically repressed as the expanding South African economy of the sixties provided proof of the benefits that accrued to whites from the government's racist exploitation of the burgeoning capitalist economy. On a trip to South Africa in 1990 to interview Nelson Mandela for a television documentary for the British Broadcasting Corporation (BBC), Miller himself identified the psychological mechanism of denial that enabled most white South Africans to ignore the pertinence of his plays to their own situation. While commenting that there was less hypocrisy about racism in South Africa than in the United States, he was nevertheless acutely aware that South Africans suffered from the "same frailties and follies" explored in his plays.[14] A concrete wall that screened the eyes of affluent whites from the spectacle of a wretched black shantytown outside Cape Town evoked for Miller the self-deception of Oedipus in Sophocles' tragedy. "Concrete walls are expensive," he stated, "but that's an investment in denial. I thought, that's the real symbol of this place—denial . . . it's like a play where people are blind to what's around them."[15]

The Crucible infiltrated the imaginations of academics, students, and serious theatergoers. By the early sixties it was not only being read and studied as an exemplary modern tragedy but, in addition to a few professional and semiprofessional productions, it was also produced at fairly regular intervals in educational establishments that included teacher training colleges, university theater departments, and technical colleges and by amateur theater groups. The earliest university production I have come across was by the Department of Speech and Drama at the University of Natal in Durban.[16] Directed by Denise Mockler, the production ran in the small proscenium arch theater at Howard College for four performances in October 1964. This department mounted no less than four productions of The Crucible over the next twenty years (1964, 1970, 1978, 1989; and its sister department, the Department of Drama Studies in Pietermaritzburg, produced the play in the eighties). A production at the Springfield Training College for Indians was directed by T. Seebadri in August 1973. In Durban during the most repressive period of the apartheid regime, The Crucible was virtually a stock play for students and anyone interested in serious drama. The play was also produced in 1971 by the University of Cape Town, and during the next twenty years by drama departments at the University of Rhodes in Grahamstown, University of the Witwatersrand, University of Pretoria, University of Stellenbosch, and at a number of high schools in different parts of the country.

Yet its direct relevance to the events of recent South African history was never explicitly alluded to by these productions. The humanist ideology of the time, in conjunction with the overt and covert levels of censorship operating in a carefully controlled state education system, necessitated the masking of overtly left-wing political discourse and supported the interpretation of Miller's plays as universal tragedies of quasi-allegorical significance.[17] John Proctor's fight to retain his integrity within a hypocritical and corrupt society went to the heart of the white liberal dilemma, yet its immediate relevance could not be explicitly stated.

At the precise moment when Athol Fugard was engaged in a sustained project that aimed to use the explicitly local historical situation of apartheid in order to express an existentialist vision of the physical and psychological cruelty of oppression and injustice, productions of *The Crucible* generalized Miller's moral analysis of corruption and political repression in such a way that South African audiences were able to remain unaware of its significance as an image of their own political circumstances. Not that this significance went entirely unnoticed. The critic of the local morning newspaper, *Natal Mercury,* speculated that there were two reasons for presenting *The Crucible* in Durban in 1964:

> Firstly, because this play by Arthur Miller is of outstanding merit.... Secondly, the play could have been chosen because of the subtle parallels which can be drawn between the Salem witch-hunts and hunts of a similar sort in this country.[18]

By the time the Speech and Drama Department at the University of Natal in Durban produced *The Crucible* again in 1970, there was even more of a gulf between the theoretically Marxist discourse of academic literature, sociology, politics, and history departments and the political apathy of the average white theatergoer. The critical reception of this production revealed little awareness of its political relevance, reflecting the success of state censorship in repressing most progressive cultural and political influences. The play was performed as an exercise in histrionics, its powerful melodramatic structure being exploited to provide an evening of highly charged emotion, glossed by Pieter Scholtz's sentimental presentation of the perennial archetype of the common man as tragic hero.

The earlier colonial respect for drama that had been validated by its prior success on the London stage was replaced by a xenophobic philistinism that was sadly reinforced by both the cultural boycott and the dominance of globalized commercial media systems. The isolation caused by the cultural and, later, the economic boycott of apartheid South Africa produced feelings of cultural inferiority and repressed political guilt. In displacing these negative feelings, the mass system of escapist entertainment encouraged theatergoers to judge serious art as boring if it attempted to articulate disturbing truths and did not mimic the snappy pace of a Hollywood movie.[19]

In 1975 *The Crucible* was directed by Barney Simon for the state-funded PACT at the Alexander Theatre in Johannesburg. Simon was something of a guru among young actors. His single-minded approach to performance made no allowance for the technical craftsmanship of the working professional. The production became legendary for the unconventional rehearsal methods that involved the actresses who were playing girls accused of witchcraft spending a night in a forest, and it seems that the production once again aimed to convey the emotional power of the experience rather than to make any trenchant comment on the state of South African society.[20] The very fact that it was produced by the state-sponsored PACT guaranteed that there could be no attempt at an overtly political interpretation. The program note emphasized seventeenth-century Salem history with no reference to McCarthyism. The director's overstated Strasbergian method approach might be seen as an attempt to compensate for the production's lack of social analysis.[21]

In postapartheid South Africa, the significance of *The Crucible* has not been lost on the theatergoing and film-going public. While assuming the play's status as a modern classic and asserting the success of Nicholas Hytner's 1997 film as an adaptation of it, a number of reviewers emphasized the relevance of Miller's drama to the realities of South Africa's recent political history:

> And there are few more powerful demonstrations of what happens when ideas and feelings are repressed by an authoritarian society than *The Crucible* . . . the film shows the tension between social order and freedom. The Massachusetts theocracy it depicts reminds one of South Africa under apartheid, a state run by those staggeringly arrogant in their ignorance and supremely confident in their tunnel vision. . . . Miller writes in the preamble to Act One of the play that "the witch-hunt was a perverse manifestation of the panic which set in among all classes when the balance began to turn towards greater individual freedom" . . . we should be wary of witch-hunts.[22]

From an African perspective, the question of witchcraft itself constitutes a major issue in a society reflecting the conflicting mentalities of African tribal religion, Calvinist theology, and Western capitalism. Maurice Podbrey's review of *Ipi Zombi,* a play about a murderous witch hunt among the black community of Kokstad in 1995, makes explicit reference to *The Crucible,* a reminder that Miller's image of witches and witch-hunting may still be as potent among certain superstitious black communities as it was among Communist-fearing whites.[23]

Although no obvious attempts were made to spell out the connection with recent South African history, the powerful impact that *The Crucible* made in Lara Foot-Newton's production for the Market Theatre in 1995 suggests that the new freedom operating in postapartheid South Africa ensured a sensitivity to its social and political significance. The director has stated that she made no attempt to signpost the relevance of the play for a South African audience; nevertheless, the performances touched spectators in personal ways. Miller's play focuses on a question uppermost in the minds of citizens in the newly democratic South Africa: What is the relationship between the demands of personal integrity and the pressures of social conformity? The fact that audiences were deeply moved by her production can be attributed in part to the increased awareness of the oppressive nature of state corruption and mob prejudice many South Africans have acquired since the end of the apartheid regime. The liberal constitution that enshrines Mandela's vision of a "rainbow nation" demands that individuals exercise exceptional personal control and that communities learn to tolerate difference even when such a strategy appears to threaten their own cultural identity. The anger and disappointment that is tangible among many communities in postapartheid South Africa constantly threatens to disrupt the fragile political compromise achieved by the ANC and to undermine hard-won personal freedoms. In South Africa *The Crucible* can apparently reflect such a sociopolitical context with startling clarity.

By the start of the new millennium, *The Crucible* had found its rightful place in South African theater as the paradigmatic drama of the struggle for personal integrity within a corrupt and repressive system. The complexity of its portrayal of the witch hunt mentality is such that it speaks to South Africans of most political persuasions, illuminating a pattern of superstition, self-interest, and prejudice that is fully recognizable to those who can now be honest about the past and the present. Reactions to the social and political meanings of *Death of a Salesman* are still rather confused and contradictory.[24] Although it is a play whose emotional impact as a domestic drama is undeniable, it seems that most white South African theatergoers are still not receptive to the devastating logic of its political critique. Sadly, economic conditions in the new South Africa are beginning to reveal its pertinence for large numbers of black South Africans in ways that make Miller's work even more prophetic.

NOTES

1. Leonard Schach championed the work of Arthur Miller, directing the premiere South African productions of *The Crucible* (Cape Town, 1956), *A View from the Bridge* (Johannesburg, Cape Town, Durban, 1958), *After the Fall* (Cape Town, 1965), and *The Price* (Cape Town, 1977). He emigrated to Israel in the late sixties but returned to South Africa occasionally to direct plays.

2. At regular intervals during the last half of the nineteenth century, actors and productions from the mother country had toured Natal and the Cape Colony, and this continued when the Union of South Africa became an independent British Commonwealth country in 1910 after the Boer War.

3. I do not believe that the cultural boycott of South Africa helped to undermine the apartheid regime. While I am convinced that both economic sanctions and the sports boycott ultimately did a great deal to pressure the white government to end apartheid, there is little doubt that the lack of genuine intellectual and cultural exchange with the outside world merely reinforced the apartheid mentality.

4. In an interview with me in August 2001, Elizabeth Sneddon, who saw the production, referred to the fact that although he was "an intelligent director," Schach demonstrated the colonial insecurity typical of white South African artists of the period by copying the productions he had admired in London.

5. In 1947 Miller had explored the world of the longshoremen in the Red Hook area as research for his screenplay, *The Hook,* and on a trip to Europe in 1948 he became acquainted with the Sicilian society that formed the milieu of the Carbones. See Enoch Brater, *Arthur Miller: A Playwright's Life and Works* (London: Thames and Hudson), 72, 76.

6. David Bloomberg's production starred Johann Nell as Willy and included one or two actors among its largely amateur cast who subsequently became professionals, including Yvonne Bryceland.

7. Joe Stewardson, who played Willy Loman in the 1975 production, was a radio and stage actor in South Africa, fairly well known for his hard drinking, macho but wryly self-deprecating image as a "rough diamond." His casting as Willy would have been somewhat against type. Linda was played by Diane Wilson. Biff and Happy were played by two young actors who later achieved great success in South Africa: Bill Flynn, who played Willy in the 2001 revival and is currently regarded as South Africa's leading male actor, and Richard Haines, who later worked for the Royal Shakespeare Company. The play was directed for PACT by Ken Leach, who used Jo Mielziner's original decor and lighting designs. This was an intense production with a skillful cast that emphasized the emotional force of the family conflicts and personal revelations. The program notes stress the play's affinity with Greek tragedy and its status as a modern classic.

8. In the end, the forces of capitalism rendered the apartheid system unsustainable and hastened its demise. Capitalism has not, however, helped the majority of black South Africans to achieve an acceptable level of material well-being, but, as in many Western countries, it has promoted a system of social discrimination based on wealth.

9. Guy Willoughby, *Cape Times,* February 2001.

10. Jim Tolley, quoted in *Death of a Salesman* media release for this production by Peter Terry.

11. A notable exception is Wilhelm Snyman's intelligent review of *Death of a Salesman,* by Arthur Miller, *Cape Times* in July 2000. He calls Willy "the archetypal victim of his own illusions" and refers to the "mendacity of the capitalist system."

12. The Treason Trial (1974–75) of a number of black consciousness leaders, including Steve Biko, was another ritual witch hunt aimed at crushing all opposition to apartheid.

13. *The Star,* 1997.

14. Christopher Wren, *New York Times,* December 6, 1990.

15. Quoted by Wren, December 6, 1990.

16. I am indebted to Professor Dennis Schauffer for information on the production.

17. It was common knowledge among the student body in most English-language universities during the sixties, seventies, and eighties that many students were employed on campuses as police informers.

18. *Natal Mercury,* October 1964.

19. Until the mid-seventies Hollywood films were the chief source of mass entertainment. A few commercial theater managements were also highly successful in producing slick versions of West End thrillers and farces and lavish productions of Broadway musicals in touring productions. It was not until 1975 that state-controlled television was introduced and became a successful palliative that had the effect of dumbing down the cultural life of the country even more successfully than commercial cinema.

20. John Proctor was played by the bilingual (Afrikaans and English) actor Marius Weyers who brought his earthy and masculine presence to the role. Weyers was characteristically bluff and visceral in his performance, combining the emotionalism that characterizes traditional Afrikaans acting styles with his own directness and simplicity as an actor.

21. Barney Simon was the artistic director of the Market Theatre from its inception in 1976 until his death in 1995.

22. *The Star,* March 7, 1997.

23. *Cape Times,* January 8, 1999.

24. There is a clear parallel with the reception of Bertolt Brecht's *Mother Courage,* a play whose critique of the contradictions of small business is often found unacceptable or simply misunderstood by liberal and humanist critics.

Michael Raab

Not All One Song
Arthur Miller in the German Theater

December 17, 1982, seemed to mark the nadir of Arthur Miller's standing in the German theater. On the evening of that day Peter Iden, the critic for the *Frankfurter Rundschau,* one of the four well-respected national dailies, entered the stalls of the Schauspielhaus in Nuremberg to attend the German premiere of *The American Clock.* The fact that no theater in Berlin, Munich, or Hamburg had tried to secure the rights for the play spoke for itself, but when Iden looked around he was surprised to see none of his usual colleagues, as the rival papers had sent only their second or third stringers. The day after his review appeared he felt obliged to justify his trip to Franconia in an additional commentary and tried to come to grips with the German theater's apparent disinterest in Arthur Miller:

> The aesthetics at least at our major theaters are far removed from the straight storytelling of an author like Miller. For this development there are many reasons. Paradoxically it is the lack of new plays that makes it difficult for the few of them still at hand to find a director's attention. That would be less hard to swallow if the audience really had followed the quantum leaps of the theater's aesthetics. But this is far from the case. In Nuremberg in the stalls you felt rather a kind of relief on the side of the spectators confronted with Miller's conventional dramaturgy. And a lot of sympathetic feeling. From the first German-speaking production in Basle one heard similar reports. How Miller describes people and their conflicts is still of interest for many.[1]

The German theater is, of course, director dominated. Despite the fact that audiences generally like a well-constructed story with compelling characters, directors tend to consider plays in terms of how much of their own vision and personality they can project into them. After all, that is what will earn them marks from the critics, enhancing their chances for further employment or even leading to the artistic directorship of a theater. A play as linear and tightly plotted as *All My Sons* is not particularly appealing to directors keen to demonstrate their own uniqueness, if need be at the cost of a text. In their attempt to be original, directors are supported by the reviewers, who all too often refer to a very good production of a well-made play as "merely solid." At worst, a critic who is unable to differentiate properly between the work of playwright, director, and actor might even insinuate that the result was mainly due to the company, imagining the director as not much more than an onlooker at rehearsals. No wonder directors who see it as their biggest achievement to disappear behind their work lead a tough existence in Germany. Rather than stage a Miller play, their publicity-conscious colleagues take on the world premiere of a half-baked new German text in the hope of getting the credit for having at least turned it into a bearable evening in the theater. Or they might deconstruct a classic, because the author is no longer protected by copyright. So if a director is keen on making a statement on bourgeois society by using the text as a springboard for his own ideas, he will not look to Miller but rather go back to one of Miller's idols: Henrik Ibsen.

The highest ambition of a director is to be invited to the Berlin Theatertreffen, where every year the previous season's most notable productions from Germany, Switzerland, and Austria are staged. To be chosen means an enormous career boost. How low playwrights rank on the scale in Berlin was illustrated by a book celebrating the festival's first twenty-five years in 1988. The index lists theaters, directors, stage and costume designers, and even the dramaturges involved, but not the playwrights. Contemporary American writers have never played a big part in Berlin. Edward Albee did relatively best with *Who's Afraid of Virginia Woolf?* (1964), *Tiny Alice* (1966), and *All Over* (1972); these productions were followed by a big gap until the production of David Mamet's *Glengarry Glen Ross* (1986) and *Oleanna* (1994). Tennessee Williams in 2000 was featured with a free adaptation of *A Streetcar Named Desire;* the regular German title, *Endstation Sehnsucht,* had to be changed into *Endstation Amerika.* The first Eugene O'Neill play invited onto the German stage for the Theatereffen was *Mourning Becomes Electra,* in 2003. German premieres have a better chance of being selected than revivals, but in Miller's case his three major plays, *Death of a Salesman, The Crucible,* and *A View from the Bridge,* all came to Germany years before the inauguration of the Theatertreffen in 1964. Still, there was at least one invitation in 1996, because from time to time a director sees a possibility in a neglected Miller work and stages it in a surprising way.

This was the case with—of all plays—*The American Clock,* in a production by David Mouchtar-Samorai from Bonn, using the new German title *Der große Knall (The Big Bang)* instead of *Die große Depression (The Big Depression).* The version used by Mouchtar-Samorai and his dramaturg Hermann Wündrich all but eliminated Miller's narrator and distributed the dialogue among eight actors and four extras, who played all the characters regardless of class or gender. The actors had to cope with up to thirteen parts. This required enormous fluency of staging, enhanced by Heinz Hauser's simultaneous set, an eerily lit blue open space with elastic white strings hanging from the ceiling, lines on the floor, and chairs becoming progressively smaller toward the back. The production was not featured on the theater's main proscenium stage but in the studio, with its rather flat acting space that proved ideal for capturing the play's tone and atmosphere. The wings were left half open to expose makeup tables and coatracks for the 140 costume changes. Hauser achieved a dreamlike impression as well as the optical equivalent of Miller's kaleidoscopic play that avoided any obvious symbolism. The production seemed to take up the author's suggestion in *Timebends* that the acting should be fast and extroverted, as in a cabaret performance. As such, it did not resemble the "mural for theater" Miller envisaged in his subtitle but rather a lightning-quick sketch. The action had a balletlike precision much helped by Dana Sapiro's choreography.

Compared to previous productions in Basel and Nuremberg, this version of *The American Clock* seemed to display a smaller, lighter, and less ponderous flashback dramaturgy; it reminded Andres Müry of "grandpa telling stories to his grandchildren and great-grandchildren by the fireside."[2] The same critic voiced his initial skepticism in an essay for *Theatertreffen Magazine 1996:* "Is that still possible? A revue-like play about the Wall Street crash and the big Depression mirrored in the history of a New York Jewish family recognizably modeled on Arthur Miller's own that—told in sentimental flashback—expresses the quintessential American belief in the human, the individual being saved in the hour of greatest need?" Yet he went on to claim that "sometimes reality works in favor of a forgotten, unfashionable play. . . . Today when capitalism, after the breaking down of the communist block has only itself as an enemy, where its clock, just like before 1929, seems to show a perpetual beginning, Miller's writing on the wall appears prophetic again. *Der große Knall,* as it is now called, accordingly can be seen as a play of the hour."[3]

Nevertheless, the production did more than merely echo the Depression, because the social malaise depicted was contrasted by the songs and jazz and swing music of the period, as well as by dance routines and comedic turns. This helped Mouchtar-Samorai avoid sentimentality; he often placed musical interludes just at the point when the economic misery of a character was at its height. During rehearsals Mouchtar-Samorai began by using improvisation before returning to the text rather late in the rehearsal process, helped as he was by Germany's generous rehearsal schedules of eight to ten weeks for a big play like *The American Clock*. With enormous confidence, his actors were able to use mime, sometimes appearing like puppets on a string or dancing with life-size puppet doubles, always reacting to the production's jump-cut dramaturgy. "Miller doesn't look at all old-fashioned any longer," wrote Andres Müry. "You just have to teach him how to dance."[4]

As a formal innovator, Miller himself plays an important role in Peter Szondi's seminal study, *Theory of Modern Drama (1880–1950),* first published by Suhrkamp in 1959. In his survey of different ways to imagine the crisis of drama, Szondi claims Miller is the unusual example of a playwright developing from imitator to innovator.[5] *All My Sons* in 1947 for Szondi still was "an attempt to salvage Ibsen's analytic criticism of society virtually unchanged for contemporary America. . . . Even that often embarrassing prop is there through which Ibsen renders visible the past in the present and that at the same time rather laboriously symbolizes the play's deeper meaning. Here it is the tree which was once planted for Larry and which by the previous night's storm had been cleft in two in the backyard where the action is set." *Death of a Salesman,* on the other hand, shows both the playwright's rapid maturity and his sophistication in the development of dramatic form. "The past is shown in the way it manifests itself in real life: as of its own volition in a Proustian *mémoire involotaire.*" Instead of a discussion about past events among various people, we have the psychological situation of an individual finding himself dominated by memory. Szondi sees the persons surrounding Willy Loman as "similar to the projected characters in expressionist drama who exist only in relation to the central me."[6] Szondi's analysis is prominently placed at the end of his influential book, giving the impression that Miller's technique was both innovative and advanced. Yet even in the year of *Death of a Salesman's* world premiere, the method was a well-known device used in film.

The same applies to Miller's use of the epic narrator, which for most German directors looks hopelessly outdated and clumsy—an attitude that drastically reduces the production possibilities for even a major Miller play like *A View from the Bridge.* As far back as the 1950s this work faced a lot of hostility from critics; it was seen as merely an individual case study without the wider resonance of *Death of a Salesman* or *The Crucible*. Nevertheless, there were at least two prestigious revivals, by Jürgen Bosse 1989 in Stuttgart and by the young director Simone Blattner at the Bavarian State Theatre in 1997. The latter in general was one of the theaters most loyal to Miller in the 1980s and 1990s, staging the premieres of *The Archbishop's Ceiling* (1987) and *Broken Glass* (1995). The former, despite being sumptuously produced, was one of the biggest critical disasters for Miller in the German theater. General opinion saw the text as well meant but harmless, full of tiresome talk, and at best a lesson for audiences with a very limited knowledge of eastern European politics. *Broken Glass* received a similarly harsh treatment. Although in Britain it received an Olivier Award, the well-cast premiere in Munich did not prove to be a critical success. Miller's champion, Peter Iden, was in a minority with the view that "the author has lost little of his ability to develop differentiated characters with his dialogue, to create climaxes and to sharply pinpoint individual scenes."[7] For Iden's younger colleagues, however, *Broken Glass* partly resembled an unintentional parody of Ibsen. Reinhard J. Brembeck claimed that "the play is not only set in 1938, it also seems written in 1938." He went on to attack the author for "needing an explanation for everything, not being able to leave things open or only allude to them. And so as usual he opens his box with the label: Ibsen-Strindberg-Freud."[8] A second production a year later at the Hamburg Kammerspiele—whose building from 1938 to 1941 housed the Jewish Cultural Association (Jüdischer Kulturbund) and for hundreds was the starting point for deportation to Auschwitz—could not redeem the play for the German repertory. Here, too, critics gave credit to Miller's undeniable craft in psychological realism, but were less convinced by his attempts to communicate new ideas.

Undaunted, the Hamburg Kammerspiele hosted the European premiere of *Mr. Peters' Connections* in 2000 with TV star Uwe Friedrichsen in the lead role. This small private theater was one of the logical homes for Miller's plays, especially for a work like *Broken Glass,* as it was for decades under the artistic directorship of Ida Ehre, one of Germany's great Jewish actresses, and after her death in 1989 continued to honor her passionate attempts to deal with the Nazi period on stage. Despite its offering one of the best parts for an older actor in recent years, municipal and state theaters were less keen on taking up *Mr. Peters' Connections.*

Ironically, in Germany Miller finds himself in a situation completely different from his problems in the American theater, which he sees as dominated by Broadway, where you can only go to "these musicals" and "entertainment shit."[9] His avowed intention in writing was always "that everybody is able to understand the plays" and that "no one needs a college education to do so." His wish to appeal to all strata of society means that the plays "contain only very few literary allusions, not too many difficult words and that the emotions are generalized."[10] In the United States, where "public subsidy is seen as Communism" and "in the theater you meet only tourists and the rich,"[11] these ideals nonetheless make him a highbrow author. In the highly subsidized German theater it is exactly his wish not to be too sophisticated that is held against Miller, and he is accused of too often stating the obvious. Being formally conventional and not especially ambiguous, however, appeals to the commercial sector in the German theater, with its older and more conservative audiences preferring modern classics to new writings that often appear too cerebral to them. Especially with touring productions, they come in large numbers to see a TV star in a well-made play by an author they know from their playguide. Therefore, with some commercial managements Miller is not only a favorite for the odd revival of *Death of a Salesman,* but even for German premieres. *The Ride Down Mt. Morgan* was first seen in Germany in 1992 at the Schauspielhaus Dresden, with a parallel opening at the Fritz Rémond Theatre in Frankfurt, a private theater normally concentrating on boulevard comedies. *The Last Yankee* in 1994 had its first production at the Renaissance Theatre in Berlin, known for offering not-too-demanding fare spiced up by the presence of actors known from TV and film. Euro-Studio Landgraf, the biggest German-speaking touring company, has committed itself to producing one Miller play per season.

In the subsidized sector Miller relies on individual directors to champion his work. Sometimes one of them even revisits a particular play. Dietrich Hilsdorf staged *The Crucible* in Ulm in 1985, took the production to Frankfurt the following season, and did a new version in 1997 in Bonn. He augmented the part of Thomas Putnam by giving him additional text based on Miller's overall narrative. The smug landowner, for example, was portrayed as the chief instigator of the girls' hysteria; whenever his interests needed to be safeguarded he appeared, whether as vox populi from the stalls or as a witness at court. Hilsdorf's imaginative staging was particularly commended for his handling of the group scenes, and his different versions of the character continued to develop in each production. With Holger Berg's two productions, however, we have the unusual example of two completely opposing interpretations of *Death of a Salesman*. His Frankfurt production in 1984 treated the play as a farce, not only heavily caricaturing the smaller roles but also entreating the audience to laugh at Willy Loman, who was shown almost as a hyperactive psycho path in need of treatment. No wonder Horst Köpke in the *Frankfurter Rundschau* bluntly stated: "I take objection to that."[12] Thirteen years later in Nuremberg, however, there was not much to laugh at; now Loman was no longer a figure of ridicule, but placed absolutely in the wrong as a thoroughly nasty and egotistical character terrorizing his family and generally getting on everybody's nerves. Berg seemed to overreact to the danger of actors either sentimentalizing Willy Loman or using the part to show their technical brilliance in playing a miserable loser. This latter course was unintentionally demonstrated by Dustin Hoffman in Völker Schlöndorff's film, which did not let you forget for a second that a major movie star was displaying his craft. Loman's suicide was rather embarrassingly played by an actor moved by his own performance. Unfortunately, this is rather common in the German theater, because so few first-rate directors take on the play, with the result that star actors merely do star turns.

Luckily this was far from the case with Jürgen Rohn in Jürgen Kruse's Bochum production in May 2001. The director's working method is to project various levels of filmic, photographic, and musical quotations and allusions over each other to form a highly complex collage. One can hardly imagine a play more suited to this approach than *Death of a Salesman*. Miller has always stressed that he doesn't use a flashback technique, but that everything happens simultaneously in Willy Loman's mind. His starting point was "the concept that nothing in life comes 'next' but that everything exists together and at the same time within us; that there is no past to be 'brought forward' in a human being, but that he *is* his past at every moment and that the present is merely that which his past is capable of noticing and smelling and reacting to," as he wrote in the introduction to his collected plays.[13] Kruse accordingly created a reverberating chamber of sounds and images overlapping in Willy Loman's mind. Chairs and tables are brought on and off stage only for the restaurant scene. Otherwise everything happens in or in front of the Loman house, with Howard, for example, simply carrying his tape recorder on a stand with him.

Despite supporters like Kruse, Berg, Hilsdorf, and Mouchtar-Samorai, Miller did not find a regular director in Germany like David Thacker in London, who did *Broken Glass* and *Death of a Salesman* at the National, *The Last Yankee* at the Young Vic, and Miller's version of Ibsen's

An Enemy of the People at the same venue. But with *The Crucible,* at least the playwright attracted the attention of a small group of directors with a strong interest in choreography, often influenced by Pina Bausch. For them the play provides an opportunity to concentrate on the psycho-sexual situation of the young girls. This was most strongly in evidence with Konstanze Lauterbach's 1999 interpretation in Bremen. Lauterbach staged an all-out attack on the spectators' senses, even using the screeching sound of a circular saw; the production created impressive stage pictures, only occasionally straining too hard to overwhelm. Yet productions like Lauterbach's demonstrate the often neglected scenic possibilities of Miller's plays.

Critical opinion about Miller's plays in the German theater remains divided to this day. Yet translations of *Death of a Salesman, The Crucible,* and *A View from the Bridge* helped to rekindle interest in the plays and in Miller's way of "caring for people often mocked and derided in the German theater."[14] In the former German Democratic Republic there weren't many prestigious Miller productions, as theaters were rarely able to afford the foreign currency for the royalties. One of the few exceptions was Wolfgang Heinz's well-cast *Incident at Vichy* at the Deutsches Theater Berlin in 1965. In 1989 the fall of the Berlin wall gave an unexpected boost to *Death of a Salesman:* when produced in the East the play was understood as a crash course in capitalism. For Miller's German agent, Uwe B. Carstensen of the S. Fischer Theaterverlag, this was "the most important development in the reception of the playwright over here for decades."[15] Due to continuously high unemployment figures in the West as well as in the East, the play received an exceptional number of productions in the 2002–3 season, notably at the Deutsches Theater Berlin, in Düsseldorf, Leipzig, and Wiesbaden (directed by David Mouchtar-Samorai).

While Miller's status in Germany as a modern classic is not in doubt, he nonetheless shares with Bertolt Brecht the fate of having critics object to too much overt didacticism. As far back as the 1950s Friedrich Luft complained about the experience of having to sit through one of Miller's plays: "Always to be told what to think creates a stubborn atmosphere in the stalls."[16] Faring better than Brecht and Miller at the present time in German theater is Samuel Beckett, who also stimulates far more academic interest. Yet, in Germany, Miller will be performed as long as any company tries to make a political statement against mass hysteria by using the parable of *The Crucible,* and as long as actors are keen to play Willy Loman, one of the archetypal characters of twentieth-century drama. More interesting for the survival of Arthur Miller in the German repertory, however, are instances like David Mouchtar-Samorai's rescuing from oblivion an unjustly forgotten text like *The American Clock* or Jürgen Kruse's very personal view of *Death of a Salesman*. Obviously, directors cannot be allowed to use the plays for gratuitous effects, but as long as theater practitioners like Mouchtar-Samorai and Kruse stay faithful to the author's intentions they should be granted the generous degree of artistic freedom that is commonplace in today's German theater. Only then can one be sure that Miller's work will not be ossified or mummified, as has been increasingly the case with Brecht's work.

NOTES

1. See *Frankfurter Rundschau,* December 21, 1982.
2. See Andres Müry, *Theater Heute,* January 1996, 50.
3. Andres Müry, *Theatertreffen Magazine 1996,* 22.
4. Müry, 23.
5. Peter Szondi, *Theory of Modern Drama, 1880–1950* (Frankfurt: Suhrkamp, 1959), 154.
6. Szondi, *Theory of Modern Drama,* 154–57.
7. See Peter Iden, *Frankfurter Rundchau,* May 11, 1995.
8. See Reinhard J. Brembeck, *tz,* May 11, 1995.
9. See *Stern,* October 2000, 213.
10. See *Frankfurter Rundschau,* January 24, 1998.
11. *Stern,* 214.
12. Horst Köpke, *Frankfurter Rundschau,* January 23, 1984.
13. See Arthur Miller, "Introduction," in *Arthur Miller's Collected Plays,* vol. 1 (New York: Viking, 1981), 1–2.
14. Knut Lennartz, *Die Deutsche Bühne,* January 2001, 3.
15. Uwe B. Carstensen in an interview with the author on May 4, 2001.
16. See Friedrich Luft, *Süddeutsche Zeitung,* April 19, 1956.

Enoch Brater

A Dominican *View*
An Interview with Darryl V. Jones

In November 1995, Darryl V. Jones directed Arthur Miller's A View *from the* Bridge *at the Source Theatre Company for a standard four-week run in Washington, DC. Enoch Brater spoke with him, on a telephone hookup arranged by WUOM-Radio on September 21, 2004, about the director's decision to reset the play in a community of Dominican immigrants.*

Enoch Brater: How did you arrive at the idea of transforming Miller's original Sicilian American Red Hook setting to a stage world inhabited by recent immigrants from the Dominican Republic?

Darryl V. Jones: At the time I had just returned to the Washington, DC, area from working at the Globe Theatre in San Diego. And it was in California that, for the first time, I became aware of the reality of an immigrant population and the idea of borders, of people coming across borders illegally. Because in San Diego you're right there on the border with Mexico, and you see the border patrol police all the time. That's when I started to think that there's another group of immigrants coming to the United States, as there always has been. I began to think not so much about Mexicans but about Latino immigration in general. Could I take this idea about the Latino community and work it into *A View from the Bridge*? I remembered that when I lived in New York in the last high-rise building on Central Park West, around W. 106th Street, I was looking down into another world, because right there on the side street there was nothing but Dominicans and Puerto Ricans. I looked like them, and when I walked down the street they would speak to me. If they spoke in Spanish, I couldn't respond. I started to reflect on that, and it made me think that perhaps my experience was similar to Arthur Miller's: a Jewish American looking down from a bridge on a community of Italians. Maybe he, too, looked like them, but he was not really part of the code of that environment. So I started to make those comparisons with my own experience, and this ultimately led to the production.

EB: How did Arthur Miller react to this idea when you discussed it with him?

DVJ: He thought it was a great idea, and he enthusiastically gave me his permission to proceed with the plan. He realized there would have to be some script changes. The major change was in Alfieri's opening monologue, because that deals with Sicilian location and exposition. We needed to adapt this to account for an appropriate Dominican family. I settled on a Dominican situation after doing a lot of research about which Caribbean country would be most similar in experience to the Italian immigration. For a long time I wanted to use Cuba, but that wouldn't work because the difference with Cuba is that you can't go back. And that's a big part of Miller's story—Marco in particular is saving money so that he can return to his wife and children. Dominicans, on the other hand, can go back and forth. We didn't want to use Puerto Rico, for example, because Puerto Rico is part of the United States—so the situation could not be the same. Eventually we settled on the Dominican perspective. Initially, when I first contacted Miller, we hadn't made this finalization. I think he liked the idea of the Dominicans because he saw that the similarities between their world and the Italians were stronger. I made a few script changes to Alfieri's opening monologue, Miller approved those changes, and we were off and running.

EB: What was your experience with Miller's work before you directed the Dominican *View?* Had you directed Miller before and, if so, how?

DVJ: No. I hadn't directed any Miller plays before. I had, of course, seen many of his plays.

EB: In your experience as an audience member, have you seen any productions of his plays which were as ambitious as yours in transforming the setting?

DVJ: No.

EB: Were you aware of any when you directed *A View from the Bridge*?

DVJ: Not at the time I was working on the production. Subsequently I found out a great deal more about this. Miller's agent told me about the famous production of *Death of a Salesman* in Beijing. They didn't change the ethnicity of the characters, but they were played by Asian actors. But I have heard through the grapevine that other productions of Miller plays have made journeys similar to mine.

EB: What were some of the challenges you faced in transforming the play from its original setting to a Dominican American ambience?

DVJ: It was actually an easy kind of transition once we got through minor script changes and the necessary plot devices to make sense with the switch in ethnicity. There was a challenge to make sure that we got the feeling and the rhythm and the sound of a Latino community versus an Italian one, so there was a sprinkling of Spanish throughout, and the "look," as you might imagine, was a little different. I also wanted to make sure that it was historically accurate, so I needed to be sure that there was actually a Latino population in Red Hook somewhere in the 1950s and 1960s, and whether or not Latinos could work on the docks. I remember being very concerned about that because the docks were, as we all know, run by the Teamsters. I knew that, because of the time, if there were Latinos working on the docks, they would of course be segregated. So I had to make sure that there actually were African Americans, that there actually were Latinos and Dominicans working as longshoremen. And in fact there were; they worked in different small shifts, and they had their own little groups. In order to make sure that this was indeed the case, we moved the time frame from the late 1940s/early '50s to 1963 or '65: we actually set it in 1964.

EB: Why did you stay with the original Brooklyn setting in Red Hook?

DVJ: I did my research early. Before we even settled on that, I went to see Red Hook for myself. Granted, this wasn't 1964, but the entire place had changed. It was—it really was—completely Puerto Rican and Dominican, and it looked as though those people had been there for quite awhile.

EB: Did you look for actors who were Dominican American, or did you use a mixed cast?

DVJ: It was a mix of African Americans and Latinos. In the role of Eddie Carbone there was a very good African American actor named Vince Brown. But we had to change some of the characters' names. Eddie stayed Eddie. We gave a Latin pronunciation to Beatrice. Catherine became Cottie. We didn't have to change Marco and Rodolpho. And that was basically it for the name changes. There were three African American actors, and everybody else in the cast was either of African Latino or white Latino background.

EB: In *A View from the Bridge* Miller makes use of popular American music, most particularly "Paper Doll." How did your production deal with that? Did you bring any Latino rhythms into the play?

DVJ: The music of the Dominican Republic is a particular kind of salsa, and I wanted to make sure we got that right. We had to bring the right Dominican sound to the show.

EB: Did you use this music in the scenes, or only as a framing device?

DVJ: It was strictly a framing device, to help establish the world of the play. I didn't use too much music during the scenes, unless it was a necessary device to help with the setting. As a matter of fact, the production opened with a big, raw, rowdy kind of street scene, as if to say, "hey, you know, we're in a different world. We're not in a little Italy, but we're still in Red Hook." And that helped to establish the world we were entering. The sound designer, Scott Burgess, was very sharp about this. All of this was important to me: I wanted to trace Eddie's evolution, his emotional evolution, through the sound design. In his case there was a sort of deterioration. I began with a more contemporary Latino music than one might have heard in 1964. But as Eddie progressed, as he became more primitive and primal in his urges, in his needs, and in his actions, the music became like a motif that followed this descent. The music evolved with him so that at the end there was nothing but the sound of bare drums. And we followed the same technique in the moment when Marco raises the chair above Eddie's head (which is one of my favorite moments in the play). There, too, we heard a more tribal and primal music that evolved from what we chose to use: not "Paper Doll" but in this case "April Love."

EB: Looking back on it now, what do you think your approach to the play accomplished, and what insights about *A View from the Bridge* do you think it revealed?

DVJ: I think it revealed a basic commonality between different people: the experience of immigrating to the United States, of being part of a larger society but still holding on to your roots. It's the aspect of learning to live in a democracy, a republic, a community that has entirely different codes of ethics and another way of doing things. I think that can basically apply to any of the immigrants who have come to the United States and stayed within a tightly knit community—and particularly the ones who end up coming over illegally, whether it be from Asia, from

Panama, from the Dominican Republic. As with all great plays, *A View from the Bridge* has a core humanity that touches and that can touch everybody. We can all recognize the relationships between Eddie and Catherine, and between Eddie and Beatrice, and among all the other characters in the play. We all know somebody or someone who's in a situation like this.

EB: What did you discover about your approach to the work as you moved through the play in rehearsal?

DVJ: Something that hit me at the time still makes a very big impression on me: one night after the show an audience member came up to me. He was a young African American man, and he said this: "Thank you so much, thank you for doing this play this way. Eddie—he's just like so many people I know. He's just like my father." I told the young man that the play was not initially done this way. And he said, "You're kidding! I thought for sure it was written to be done this way." What really hit me was that the the play can really transcend race. That was a real pat on the back! People didn't even know that I had done anything to the play.

EB: In developing your conception for this production, and in the process of working on it with your cast, did you discover things about the play that were rough edges, or that were real challenges, or that were, in some unforeseen way, remarkable revelations?

DVJ: I think one of the things I discovered is that I wanted to see more of Bea—a little bit more of her dilemma and her struggle. So after the scene she has with her niece Catherine, where she basically says, "Honey, you gotta leave, you gotta get out of here," I staged a silent moment. I left Bea on stage, and I had her pray to the Madonna; and then she started hitting herself—"mea culpa, mea culpa, my fault, my fault." I wanted to show how painful all of this was for Beatrice and how this whole moment was hers. I think if anything I may have elevated her role in the play. What I discovered is that I wanted very much to tell more of her story.

EB: That's very essential to the play. As you know, when Miller revised *A View from the Bridge* from its original one-act version to the two-act work we know in the theater today, he spent a lot of time trying to expand the women's roles in the play. I still think audiences today want to see more of that.

DVJ: I hope I can take a little credit for this. But I have a tendency to want to tell the women's story. I just wanted my production to tell a little bit more. One of the things I think I did wrong occurred in the scene between Eddie and his two fellow longshoremen. They had a scene on the stoop leading up to Eddie's house. And they tease him about Rodolpho. They made it look as though Rodolpho was very limp wrist, that Rodolpho was gay—it was much too obvious. After I staged it this way I realized that this was completely off key. All of this is much more interesting if all of this is in Eddie's head. It's important to see them saying that Rodolpho is a fun guy—he sings a lot, he dances. It is Eddie who twists things around. That's a more revealing choice, but it's not the one I made at the time.

EB: Would you consider, as a director, the same approach of crossing ethnic lines in any other Miller play?

DVJ: Well, in *Death of a Salesman* this wouldn't matter at all. It's harder to do this if it's something that's based in history. But it certainly can be done with any play that's character driven. Part of me says all of this has been done before, especially in the 1960s and '70s, when nontraditional casting became something of a buzzword. Actually, there's been less of this in recent years, with the exception of Shakespeare, and I don't know the reason for that. Perhaps it's because people are producing more African American plays. Sometimes there's a backlash from the African American community: "Well, it's great that you did that, that's wonderful—but let's do plays by black writers." But I would cross those ethnic lines again: the more we can show how close we all are—all of us, regardless of who wrote the play—that's the point for me.

EB: What advice, if any, would you give to directors seeking to situate Miller's plays in a variety of American communities?

DVJ: The first advice would be to make sure that what you're doing is historically accurate. If you're going to stage it black, make sure that there was indeed a black population in wherever it is you're going to stage it. The other advice would be to make sure that you accurately create the world of the play: pay particular attention to the world Miller put down in the text, his indication for the setting, and only then consider whether or not it needs to be altered. Trust the play: that's my main piece of advice. One of the reasons I chose *A View from the Bridge* as one of my earliest professional productions is that I remembered what a very wise teacher told me when I was in graduate school: "Half the battle, more than half the battle, is starting with a great play. You start with a great play and a lot of your work is done." So I would say to other directors, especially young ones, trust the play, create the right world for it, and don't feel as though you have to change it. Enhance the playwright's intentions, but don't change his or her intents.

EB: In terms of transforming the setting of the play, or in switching ethnicities, just how far do you think directors might be able to go?

DVJ: In the case of *A View from the Bridge*, I didn't have to change the location, and I think that helped the production a lot. I thought about a setting in Miami, or someplace else, but ultimately came to the conclusion that this would be doing too much to the play. Less is more. I really believe that if you can change the ethnicity while leaving the plays where they are, perhaps moving them up in time, this goes a long way in showing the cultural shifts in America. If you leave something someplace, but you now see a different ethnic group living there, the cultural change speaks for itself. If you change the place as well as the ethnicity and the race, it might be more than the play can bear. Then again, it would certainly depend on the production. Who knows? It might just work. It's always easier to do this with Moliére or Shakespeare or Shaw, because they're much further away in time.

EB: How did your second production of *A View from the Bridge* differ from the show you did at the Source Theatre in Washington?

DVJ: In October 2000, as part of the University of Michigan symposium in honor of Miller's eighty-fifth birthday, I was approached by the chair of the Department of Theatre and Drama, Erik Fredricksen, about the possibility of directing the play. I was on the faculty at that time, and I remember that we talked about doing the play when you were organizing the symposium.[1] My first instinct was to try to re-create the Dominican production I had done in Washington, this time using students in the program. But when it came to cast it there simply weren't enough students of color to cast it this way. The one student of color who might have been right for Eddie was doing another show. So we went back to the Italian version, and I have to say that going back to the original version deepened my appreciation for the play. I think that I saw more of the play the second time around. I decided to submerge the cast in the research I had done about the Sicilian American community. I did lots of book research, lots of film research, and lots of sound research because I wanted to depict truthfully a group of people different from my own ethnic background. This was also new territory for the student actors. Even though we all had a great deal of exposure to the Italian American community through films and television, I still needed to know more about this to get it right. If I were white and had to direct a black play, I suppose I would have to do the same thing. The more I researched, and the more I worked on the play for the second time, the more my understanding of the characters grew. That is one reason I think I got the scene with Eddie and his fellow longshoremen right this time. I think I was able to focus more on the play itself, on who the characters were, and also on Alfieri's relationship to the story. In my first production I was more concerned with making sure that the change I made was justified, and that all of this worked. The second time around I didn't have to worry about changing the play. All I had to do was focus on telling the story, and this deepened my appreciation for the characters and the structure of the drama.

EB: What were the challenges you faced in working with students after directing the play with a professional cast in Washington?

DVJ: At Michigan we had some really good and smart young actors. Of course, there's a difference, because you're looking at everybody who's the same age in school, supposedly playing a range of ages, so there's always something here that strikes you as slightly untrue. But once you get beyond that these kids did a terrific job. Honestly, there wasn't a tremendous amount of difference in working with the two casts. If anything, I had to hold the students back because this play is like a speeding train; sometimes student actors go further than seasoned actors, only because they haven't learned the skill of holding back. They haven't learned the boundaries and every now and then they go a little too far. But they really were smart and well trained and I'm not saying that because I was part of the department at that time. That's really the truth.

EB: Did you use a mixed cast for this production?

DVJ: Yes. Because I couldn't do a Dominican production, I decided to do color-blind casting. Marco, for example, was played by Boyd Wright, an African American student in the program. He was simply the best actor for the role.

EB: How did you get the students from so many different backgrounds to understand that they had to live in the Italian atmosphere of Miller's play?

DVJ: I used some of the same devices I used in Washington, because even at the Source Theatre most of my actors had to "be" Dominicans even if they were not Dominicans. In Ann Arbor, as in Washington, I used a lot of photos. I really wanted them to see the people, to relate to them and finally say, "Yes, that's the essence of my character right there." I wanted the actors to engage their senses visually. In Washington I also did this with sound, to help the actors establish the Dominican world of the production. Sound helped to place them "there." With the students I did walking exercises: What do you smell as you walk through Red Hook? Do you smell the sea air? Do you smell the fish? Do you smell the tomatoes and the garlic? Lots of improvisations!

EB: Has your experience with the two productions of *A View from the Bridge* whetted your appetite for doing more Miller, in either a straight or an adaptive way?

DVJ: The answer's yes. I would love to do more Miller, and it doesn't really matter to me whether it's the way he wrote it or whether it's an adaptation. They're just such wonderful plays to get ahold of. It's so nice to direct things that work! He says so many things that are political, but you forget that you're hearing politics because you're so interested in watching his people. That's why I love these plays—he's saying things to me and he's saying them through people I care about. And it's not just rhetoric.

EB: Did Miller ever see your Dominican production?

DVJ: Unfortunately, not. We did speak about it and of course we discussed the script changes through faxes and telephone calls. He spoke about the Dominican production when he lectured at Oxford University in the United Kingdom. After our initial communications, I mostly discussed my work on the play with his agent.

EB: What do you think is the most important thing you learned from your own Dominican *View?*

DVJ: That there's a great opportunity here to open up Miller's plays in new directions, to see things in them that we might not see if we only did them "straight."

NOTE

1. See Enoch Brater, ed., *Arthur Miller's America: Theater and Culture in a Time of Change* (Ann Arbor: University of Michigan Press, 2005), vii–viii.

RETROSPECTIVES

Matthew Martin

Arthur Miller's Dialogue with Ireland

Any discussion of Arthur Miller in connection with Ireland falls into two halves, for it has been—both explicitly and implicitly—a dialogue. Miller's dialogue with Ireland has included both his own work interpreted on the Irish stage as well as the Irish dramatic tradition influencing his own dramatic practice. The latter culminated in his 1998 decision to ask one of the country's leading directors, Garry Hynes of the Druid Theatre Company in Galway, to direct the off-Broadway debut of his play *Mr. Peters' Connections.* Yet Hynes's involvement with Miller's career is by no means the first example of the playwright's Irish connection. Irish theatrical achievement, in Miller's mind, has been understood at times to be on a par with that of the New York–based Group Theatre, which we commonly cite as one of the early influences on his career.

In *Timebends* Miller talks of having had his "brain branded by the beauty of the Group Theatre's productions" in the 1930s. He writes that he was attracted by "the sheer physical spectacle of those shows, their sets and lighting . . . and the special kind of hush that surrounded the actors, who seemed both natural and surreal at the same time." There is only one other group of actors and one other production style—those of Dublin's Abbey Theatre—to which he can compare the work of Elia Kazan, Luther and Stella Adler, and the sets and lighting of Boris Aronson and Mordecai Gorelik:

> When I recall them [the Group Theatre], time is stopped. They seem never to have been tempted to make an insignificant gesture. The closest to these productions that I ever saw was the Abbey Theatre's *Juno and the Paycock* with Sara Allgood and Barry Fitzgerald, who humbled the heart as though before the unalterable truth.[1]

Ireland and Irish theater have remained in Arthur Miller's consciousness; he kept himself up-to-date on developments in Irish theater and
told Enoch Brater in 2000 that "the best work being done for the
stage today is being produced by the young Irish playwrights."[2] Miller,
in turn, has become a prominent presence in Irish culture largely due
to the inclusion of his work in the syllabi for state-run literature exams
at the secondary level. As in Israel, it would be unusual to find a student
of literature in Ireland who has not read either *The Crucible* or *Death of
a Salesman*.

Productions of Miller plays are, then, bankable for theater companies
in Ireland, North and South, because of the guaranteed student trade
at the box office. *The Crucible,* particularly, accounts for a number of
regional tours, amateur productions, and regional company productions
in Ireland. However, Miller's work accounts for few startling or memorable moments in the history of the Irish stage. As Hynes said of the significant place Miller holds in her own theatrical consciousness, "He was
someone I was always aware of and deeply admired—but largely through
my contact with his work on the page." When asked if she can remember
any particularly groundbreaking productions in Ireland of Miller's work,
her answer is terse: "No. We don't have a great history here of doing
American drama."[3]

It was Hilton Edwards and the Gate Theatre who were responsible
for first bringing Miller's work to Ireland. In 1951, the first Irish production of *Death of a Salesman* occurred at a time when all Gate productions
were taking place in Dublin's Gaiety Theatre, while their home space
was being leased in an effort to ward off growing financial worries. The
play was, even in 1951, slightly ahead of its time as far as Irish theater
was concerned. It was met with mixed reviews. The *Irish Independent* was
delighted with Edwards's handling of the staging but felt the play lacked
substance. The final judgment seemed to be that Irish theatrical production values won out over the hollowness of this American play's materialist themes. According to Seamus Kelly, who reviewed the production for
the *Irish Independent,* Edwards didn't manage to save the playwright in
his debut in Ireland:

> Hilton Edwards's gift for the mechanics of production only
> seems to emphasize the barrenness of this American "success"
> with an audience not inclined to regard suicide as something
> debatable as a twenty-thousand dollar investment for one's fam-
> ily, or spirituality as the clichés of expediency, drawled out with

a cynical leer by a ghost in a lounge suit. [Happy and Biff] complete this rather obnoxious family.[4]

This fundamentally anti-American commentary is, when placed in its historical and cultural context, susceptible to a reading of its own. When, in
1951, Kelly calls Miller's play an American "barren success," a clear judgment is being passed on more than a theatrical effort. Miller's "obnoxious family" symbolizes for this reviewer the wrong path just beyond his
own country's cultural crossroads. From the point of view of an Ireland
pained by its own cultural crisis,[5] Willy Loman's death cannot be granted
the dignity of a tragic framework. The spiritual emptiness of Willy's life,
from the point of view of Ireland in the 1950s, is not in itself a tragedy;
it is rather the obstacle preventing Willy's dilemma from attaining tragic
proportions. The great heroic Irish theatrical tradition does its best to
bring stature to the play, but in vain.

Conservative Ireland put forth other objections to Miller's play,
objections that raised hopes in some people of another momentous dis-
pute in Irish theatrical history; and that nearly put Miller's name down
in Irish theatrical annals right next to that of his much-admired Sean
O'Casey.[6] Reactionary protesters outside the theater on opening night
were deployed by "The Catholic Cinema and Theatre Patrons' Association."
Their pamphlet objected to Miller's alleged membership in such organi-
zations as the American Youth for Democracy, the Civil Rights Congress,
the People's Institute of Applied Religion, Inc., the Progressive Citizens of
America, the Stage for Action, the World Federation of Democratic Youth,
and the Voice of Freedom Committee, all of which were cited as subversive by the House Committee on Un-American Activities. The play's
own antimaterialist message, while lost on the protesters, was not lost by
the *Irish Independent* review, which noted that it was unable to "detect the
hidden hand of Joseph Stalin anywhere in its text."[7]

The Crucible appeared for the first time in Ireland in 1960, directed
by Barry Cassin. The 37 Theatre Company, so named for its venue—
a basement at 37 Baggot Street, Dublin—was granted the rights to the
play. "Quite surprisingly, really," says Cassin:

We were a small theatre company, and just why we would
have been able to do the play first, as opposed to all the bigger
theatre companies in Dublin is unclear—although I have a
two-fold theory. The significance of the play was probably not
really recognized in Ireland at the time. McCarthyism didn't

strike home in the Irish mind then. And even if it had, one had
to recognize that most of the Irish Catholic populace would
have been quite opposed to communism anyway. It wasn't until
later productions in Ireland came along, for younger generations, that the play really caused a stir. But I've always been a
devotee of the play—and when there were three simultaneous
productions in 1995, I saw each one—Dublin, Waterford, and
Belfast.[8]

As Cassin points out, 1995 was a remarkable year for *The Crucible*
in Ireland—a much-changed Ireland from the 1960s. The play was now
received with a great deal more interest and enthusiasm. In the interim
there had been the Abbey revival of the play in 1978 under the direction of Eugene Lion, a production that was not well received. Aside from
problems of pacing and an inadequate solution for dealing with the problem of accents, this 1978 production also failed to resonate with any contemporary issues. Whereas Miller himself says successful performances of
The Crucible are an indicator of those places where something significant
is going to happen in a country's political culture, the lukewarm reception of the Abbey production was itself a reflection of a moment of
political passivity. While Northern Ireland had been tearing itself apart
through civil strife for more than a decade, the South remained largely
uninvolved. As Terence Brown has observed,

> The Northern conflict therefore did not stimulate major ideo-
> logical redirection in the Republic. Throughout a decade of
> violence and political vacuum in the six counties the Southern
> state maintained its commitment to economic and social prog-
> ress, apparently ignoring when it could the commotion at its
> doorstep.[9]

In 1978 Miller's play might have been, culturally speaking, a mistimed
choice for the Abbey. There seemed to be little public sense that the play
contained an implicit commentary on the state of the Republic as it
went about its commercial concerns. Donal Foley, writing in his Saturday
column for the *Irish Times,* seems hard-pressed to find an Irish analogy to
the Salem witch trials:

> Arthur Miller, in his interesting programme note, also tells us
> a little of what happened in Salem after the executions. . . .

Certain farms which had belonged to the victims were left to ruin, and for more than a century no one would buy them or live on them. The kind of thing which happened in Ireland after some evictions.[10]

Foley's tone seems to suggest there was only a tenuous connection between this production and the current Irish context. Ironically, at the very same time another Miller play was struggling to capture the North's attention in Belfast. *All My Sons* was a critical commentary on just the sort of commercial determination driving the South, but the war-torn North had little time for discussing such insights:

> *All My Sons* which opened last week at the Lyric is a disappointing production.... For a start, to a generation who have witnessed Watergate and, nearer home, daily doorstep murders, the theme doesn't really appall. We feel disapproval—but not outrage.[11]

Each play might have had a greater chance of provoking a response had it been performed in the other's venue; for each makes a commentary more pointedly directed at the other national context. One might even conclude that both theaters were playing it safe by avoiding commentary on their immediate social and political contexts.

By 1995, however, Ireland had virtually an entire year of social commentary presented to it through Miller's work—all of it focused through the lens of *The Crucible*. In April 1995, the Abbey mounted a production of *The Crucible* under the direction of John Crowley. Ireland, North and South, had seen a great deal of political change, progress, and conflict in the previous five years as the peace process brought all players around one table. The Irish taoiseach and the British prime minister were increasingly being seen issuing joint press statements, and various factions of unionism and nationalism were engaging in dialogue within their own ranks and across the political divide. Irish cultural and national identity were the topic of tense discussion and analysis. And what had seemed a dreary, detached play on the same Abbey stage seventeen years earlier suddenly struck audiences as a crucial piece of theater:

> Here is none of your mere theatrical pabulum where a few minutes watching or listening will produce a momentary tear or a quick laugh.... Here are the searing anger, the sustained

intellect, the clear, vivid writing, the tearing emotion, the consistent demand for close attention, and the determined and undemonstrative directorial vision to allow the author to speak through the actors, which enables true human tragedy to provide catharsis through drama.[12]

The Republic of Ireland was, largely in light of the developing awareness of issues in the North, undergoing a period of intense cultural and political self-analysis. The peace process in the North had largely hinged on a close scrutiny of the South's constitutional commitment to a united Ireland, while other controversial issues in the South, including the legality of divorce and abortion, were also being widely debated.

> One of the reasons why this play was appropriately chosen for staging here by the Abbey at this time might have something to do with the uncritical righteousness which exists now in this country in respect of debates on such issues as abortion and divorce.[13]

The passion with which Nowlan writes about this production serves to highlight just how energized and contentious the cultural-political debate was in Ireland in the mid-1990s.

Just three months later, the small but highly esteemed Red Kettle Theatre Company in Waterford launched its own production of *The Crucible*. The chronological proximity of the two productions—and the geographical distance between them—were interpreted in Irish cultural circles as a clear statement about the significance of regional theater and its ability to challenge the Abbey for the rights to national prominence. The *Irish Times* itself acknowledged the competition:

> The Abbey Theatre, only a few months ago, mounted a production of Arthur Miller's *The Crucible* which had the critics, with rare unanimity, reaching for their superlatives. Even those who consider, as I do not, that comparisons are odious might concede that a new production, so soon after, must be challenged by such a precedent. The Red Kettle company's version . . . picked up the gauntlet and wove its own superb tapestry from the same materials. . . . The acting, generally, is near-flawless . . . [and] production values are well up to the standards which have earned Red Kettle a national reputation.[14]

The *Cork Examiner* took note of the challenge as well, and registered the company's success:

> Red Kettle has passed its severest test in ten tough years in theatre. The Waterford-based company's production of *The Crucible* . . . compares favourably, and in a few aspects surpasses the acclaimed Abbey production earlier this summer. It was a hiding to nothing situation if Red Kettle did not match the incredible standards set by the National Theatre in the Arthur Miller classic. This sense of being second into the theatrical ring served only to heighten the usual sense of occasion.[15]

The Crucible was being used in this year as the yardstick by which Irish theater companies measured themselves. And just as the Abbey's dominance was coming under threat from Waterford to the south, so a similar challenge was being mounted from the north. Belfast threw its hat into the ring and mounted a similarly successful production in a season of outstanding *Crucibles.* The London *Sunday Times* took note of the depths in Miller's play that allowed a third company to enter into an increasingly crowded competition:

> As if to punch home the *ritual* aspect of theatre, the critic's third implacable *Crucible* this year saw him trawling again through the symphony of Arthur Miller's extraordinary, distanced moral equation, yet still finding new gems of enlightenment; its beautiful narrative and sociological layering making it one of those plays you can watch again and again.[16]

The Belfast production received equally laudatory notices and equally energized commentary regarding the social implications of doing such a play in such a place and at such a time.[17]

Just as Miller's work brought into relief some of the key tensions within the Irish dramatic tradition back in the 1950s, so his work served in the 1990s as a vehicle through which Irish theater companies sharpened their skills in competition with one another. In the battle of the *Crucibles,* Miller was keenly aware of the role his work played in its specifically Irish context. It was his visit to the Galway-based Druid Theatre in 1997, after all, that brought him into contact with Garry Hynes, who took on the job of directing *Mr. Peters' Connections* in New York just three years after the popularity of all three *Crucibles* in Ireland.

Ireland has maintained a constant space for Miller's work on its stages, even though, as Hynes has implied, Ireland has not yet mounted a production that has had a major impact in terms of the world's understanding of Miller. Nevertheless, Ireland's dialogue with Miller has been fruitful both for Ireland's understanding of its own theatrical tradition and for Miller's understanding of its relationship to his own dramatic practice.

NOTES

1. See Arthur Miller, *Timebends: A Life* (New York: Grove Press, 1987), 230.

2. Arthur Miller in conversation with Enoch Brater, October 26, 2000, as reported to the author.

3. Garry Hynes in an interview with the author, August 27, 2001.

4. Seamus Kelly, "American Play Is a Barren Success," *Irish Independent,* April 14, 1951, 4.

5. For a discussion of this point, see Terence Brown, "Stagnation and Crisis," in *Ireland: A Social and Cultural History, 1922–1985* (London: Fontana Press, 1981), 180–82.

6. On this issue concerning the Irish premiere of *Death of a Salesman* in relation to the famous *Playboy* riots and those surrounding *The Plough and the Stars,* see Quidnunc, "An Irishman's Diary," *Irish Times,* April 4, 1951, 4.

7. Kelly, "American Play," 4.

8. Barry Cassin in an interview with the author, February 15, 2002.

9. See Brown, "Stagnation and Crisis," in *Ireland,* 182.

10. Donal Foley, "The Saturday Column," *Irish Times,* March 10, 1978, 12.

11. C. McQ., "Theatre," *Sunday News,* October 8, 1977.

12. David Nowlan, "Power Play," *Irish Times,* March 10, 1978, 10.

13. Nowlan, "Power Play," 10.

14. Gerry Colgan, "Red Kettle's Classic *Crucible,*" *Irish Times,* July 13, 1995.

15. Declan Hassett, "*The Crucible* a *tour de force,*" *The Cork Examiner,* July 13, 1995.

16. See the review of *The Crucible,* by Arthur Miller, *The Sunday Times,* October 8, 1995.

17. For other reviews of the Belfast production of *The Crucible,* by Arthur Miller, see Charles Fitzgerald, "Miller Exposes the Depths of Damnation," *Belfast Newsletter,* October 2, 1995; Grania McFadden, "Miller's Classic Gem Gets a Little Extra Sparkle," *Belfast Telegraph,* September 29, 1995; and Jane Coyle, "Allegory Laid Bare," *Irish Times,* October 2, 1995.

John T. Dorsey

Miller, Mingei, and Japan

Cultural contacts and transactions are often determined by chance: when we consider the dramatic contingencies of translation, production, reception, political climate, social situation, and publication practices, the possibilities for failure seem unlimited, especially in dealing with two cultures so different from each other as those of Japan and America. Writing about the difficulties faced by Japanese actors performing in Western plays, Peter Arnott observed, "The gulf between the Japanese theatre and its Western counterpart embraces more than different social standards and unfamiliar subject-matter. They are two forms built on different aesthetic foundations, and divided by the actor's concept of his relation to his role. The extrovert and presentational style cultivated for centuries in Japan cannot be easily reconciled with plays written for actors trained in a different mode and expected to identify themselves psychologically with their roles."[1] This seems to be an overstatement of the case, especially when we consider that *shingeki,* the "new" or Western theater in Japan, is already nearly a hundred years old. And in the case of Arthur Miller productions in Japan, we have a particularly good tale to tell, for many of Miller's plays have been produced successfully, and the major works have been revived repeatedly for over fifty years.

One major factor in the production of Arthur Miller plays in Japan is the Theater Troupe of Mingei. The word *mingei,* which usually refers to folk art, is used here in a broad sense to mean theater for the people; one of the early slogans of the group was in fact a "theater for everyone."[2] The emphasis of this theater group from the outset has been on drama that is socially relevant. According to the "Production Record of the Mingei Theater Group," it was originally established in 1947 under the name Minshu Geijutsu Gekijo by Kubo Sakae as an attempt to establish a theater of realism and to maintain liberalism and conscience after the war; but after a few years the group disbanded because of financial pressures and political disagreements. It was reorganized in 1950 as Gekidan Mingei with founding members including the actors and stage directors Uno Jukichi (1914–88) and Takizawa Osamu (1906–2000). The former was the leader of Mingei from 1954; he performed in many of their productions, playing the role of Biff in the first Japanese production of *Death of a Salesman* in 1954. Thus the Mingei theater group has been producing plays by Miller, and had regular contact and cooperation with the author, for over half a century.[3]

Closely associated with the Mingei theater group from the outset was director Sugawara Takashi. Beginning with his Japanese language version of *Salesman,* Takashi continued to translate most of the works by Miller produced by Mingei until his death in May 1970. It was Kurahashi Ken, however, who published a five-volume collection of Miller's work that is still the standard translation in Japan.[4] After Takashi's death, Kurahashi began to work closely with the Mingei theater group in the translation of Miller's texts for the Japanese stage.

Between September 1945 and April 1952, Japan was subject to the American occupation, which had widespread effects on Japanese culture.[5] During this period the Americans wanted to introduce the Japanese to U.S. culture, while at the same time monitoring elements of dissent. In regard to the introduction of American theater in Japan, the cultural wing of the American occupation at first encouraged the reading and translating of works by Tennessee Williams and Arthur Miller, but later discouraged dissemination of their plays because they showed America in a negative light. In the theater, the desire to keep tabs on undesirable tendencies in Japan led to the banning of Japanese works, at first those considered right-wing and militaristic, and later those considered left-wing and Communist, particularly with the phase beginning in June 1950 known as the Red Purge. Thus, those who had been persecuted during the war for their left-wing views were championed as opponents of militarism immediately after the war and felt liberated; during the Red Purge they faced a new, if less intense, round of persecution. In particular, with the start of the Korean War, shingeki actors, including members of the Mingei theater group, were considered Communists or Communist sympathizers, and they faced blacklisting by the film industry, by NHK Broadcasting, and even by commercial theaters. The records of the Mingei group report that they even ran into trouble putting on a production of Anton Chekhov's *The Seagull,* and the group was temporarily banned from performing in either Tokyo or Osaka. The occupation ended in April 1952, in accord with the San Francisco Peace Treaty, just as America was caught up in the growing storm of anti-Communist hysteria that would briefly threaten Miller in his own country. The production of *Salesman* in 1954 in Japan, therefore, was partly made possible by the end of the American occupation.

Another important factor that affects the reception of a foreign work is the cultural readiness of the theater group and its audience. The Mingei theater group had devoted itself to social or political plays from the outset, and it was naturally attracted to Miller's repertory. Like other groups devoted to modern theater or shingeki, Mingei was familiar with Henrik Ibsen and Maxim Gorky and with naturalistic plays based on works by, among others, the Japanese novelist Shimazaki Toson. The company was thus prepared for Miller in terms of his realistic social drama, and it looked to his work for inspiration in an effort to create a theater of realism in Japan. The postwar mission of Mingei came in fact from studying *A View from the Bridge,* which suggests, among other things, that society is not what it is but what people have made it.

Let us look at the translations of the titles of Miller's plays in order to get a sense of the cultural complexities involved in rendering his work into Japanese. In the translation of *Salesman* the word *salesman* is transliterated, that is, simply transcribed using one of the Japanese syllabary systems that is often used for foreign words. In 1954 there were, as there still are, salesmen in Japan, but the image of the traveling salesman as a solid, middle-class representative of America's expanding economy does not correspond to the image of a salesman in Japan.[6] A more relevant equivalent, pointing squarely at the middle class and touching the roots of the "Japanese dream," would be the transliterated English words *salary* and *man,* which are difficult to pin down in English and mean something like a white-collar worker or office worker. These representatives of Japan's expanding economy in the 1960s, 1970s, and 1980s were widely caricatured abroad as the traveling samurai of Japanese companies, and many of them in the sales division indeed might travel from place to place, showing the line of products, representing their companies, and opening up new territories both within Japan and elsewhere. They devoted themselves to their companies, and when many of them lost their jobs in the late 1980s and 1990s, there was an equivalent shock to the Japanese dream of middle-class life. Thus, since its first production in 1954, *Salesman* has become increasingly relevant to subsequent generations in Japan; so much so, that even students today react to it as the story of their own fathers or as the cautionary story of the "salaryman" future that awaits them. In our own century, however, the word *salesman,* transliterated into Japanese, has taken on the same meaning it had in its original American text.

The title of *The Crucible* has been directly translated into Japanese as a clay or porcelain vessel used in scientific experiments to melt, break down, or purify materials through heat. This image, however, does not resonate with Japanese audiences, lacking as it does those Latin-derived associations with such words as crucial, excruciating, and crucify, which animate a word that is unfamiliar in English as well. In one production, a subtitle was added in Japanese, "the witches of Salem," similar to the title of the French film script made by Jean-Paul Sartre. This made things somewhat clearer, of course, except for the unfamiliarity of the town name and the lack of witches in Japan.[7] Fortunately, perhaps, teachers of American culture in Japan at one stage seized upon the concept of Puritanism as a fundamental explanation for much of what takes place in America, just as Americans have seized upon the much more slippery concept of Zen Buddhism in order to explain Japan. And as this insight into American culture became widespread in Japan, *The Crucible* became, oddly enough, more accessible as a work for the theater. Inasmuch as the Puritans in the play were associated exclusively with Americans, however, the implications of the play presented further complications for Japanese audiences. Students in Japan have much more difficulty understanding this play than *Salesman,* except of course for its love story, a feature very appealing in the 1996 film version of the play, starring Daniel Day-Lewis as Proctor.

Translating words and ideas from one language to another is one problem, but translating words and ideas to the stage is another, and this brings us to one aspect of production in Japan that overlaps with the number of concerns mentioned by Miller in *Salesman in Beijing.* The subject is a difficult one because it concerns concepts and images of race and racial features. One question that Miller asks a number of times in his book is: Where is the play supposed to be taking place? In America? In China? Or perhaps in an imaginary country, as Miller describes it, "a sort of new and undiscovered country where none of us had been before—they in their imaginary Willy-Loman America and I in a Chinese Brooklyn."[8] Initially Miller was determined to veto the use of colored wigs and other apparatus intended to transform Chinese actors into white Americans: "In other words," he wrote, "they are intending to 'whiten' themselves for the play."[9] In the end he came to accept some modified attempts because he recognized that the expectations of the Chinese audience had to be taken into account.

In Japan, at one stage of the development of the modern theater, foreign works were actually called "red hair plays," referring to the light or brown hair of foreigners. Wigs, dyed hair, heavy makeup, and rubbery putty noses were common. And, in productions in the 1950s and 1960s especially, this type of "red hair" foreigner was the rule rather than the exception. For example, reporting on Japanese productions in the 1960s, Peter Arnott writes, "Many a production sags under the weight of nose-putty. A play like Arthur Miller's *Incident at Vichy,* which has French and German characters, a gipsy and a Jew, calls on every method of facial disguise the actor knows."[10] Although such attempts may seem to Americans a crude form of racism or a curious form of cultural colonization, we should take into account that wigs and other accoutrements would have seemed much less alienating to Chinese and Japanese audiences; they were familiar with the conventions of their respective traditional theater forms in which wigs, heavy makeup, and even masks were used in a system of symbolic signification. Arnott concludes that "old habits die hard. Although few modern actors have any close connection with *kabuki,* they preserve, instinctively, the traditions by which the Japanese theater was for so long bound."[11]

More recent Miller productions in Japan have found it less necessary to resort to imitating ethnicity and specific racial features in order to perform his plays. Partly as a result of the hegemonic Americanization of Japan, or the globalization of both Japan and America, audiences are now able to understand that even with openly Japanese actors, the literal background of a Miller play is indeed America—but they are also able to feel that it could take place in their own country, in their own city, even in their own home. The program for the second production of *Salesman* in 1957 even noted that in the years since 1954 the Japanese social situation and its business culture had become very close to the United States—concepts like "neurosis," "monthly payments," and "manager sickness" had already become surprisingly familiar. And by 1975, in a review by Miyagishi Yasuji, who remembered the original 1954 production, there is even some nostalgia for a Japan that could be seen in opposition to the America represented by the occupation and for the political tension that existed between the lately occupied Japan and the still influential if not dominating power of America. On the other hand, he observes that in the intervening years, life in Japan has become so much like that in America that *Salesman* can be taken as a personal story of life in Japan rather than as a political analysis of forced proximity.[12] During my twenty-five years in Japan, I have noticed how comfortable audiences have become with the settings, customs, and conventions of European and American plays, especially contemporary urban ones that seem to be taking place in London and Tokyo, or Tokyo and New York. Indeed, a New York–based play may be better welcomed and understood in Tokyo than in some parts of America.

Considering these factors, it seems clear that Miller has been quite fortunate in Mingei's choice of director, Sugawara Takashi, and in one of the group's main actors, the late Takizawa Osamu. Sugawara went to New York to study and later to see productions and the early film of *Salesman;* still later he worked on creating Japanese subtitles for the film. He made careful notes not only for the actors but also for the audience. He also directed plays by American playwrights Eugene O'Neill (*Desire Under the Elms,* 1957) and Tennessee Williams (*The Glass Menagerie,* 1959) and plays by Ibsen *(An Enemy of the People* and *A Doll House),* Gorky *(The Lower Depths),* and Chekhov *(The Seagull).* Opinions are still divided on how closely he modeled his productions on the originals and how much creativity and originality were involved in the process. To some observers, Japanese productions of Western plays, including Miller's, even now tend to be a little too close to the originals in terms of staging, lighting, costumes, and sets.

The actor Takizawa Osamu, however, was well known for his sensitive performance of Willy Loman in the first Japanese production (1954); and he revived his interpretation a number of times, later acting as director after Sugawara's death. He also played in a number of other Miller works, including the roles of Danforth in the original production of *The Crucible* (1962) and Eddie in *A View from the Bridge* (1960).

The Mingei theater group not only produces groundbreaking programs for its audience but sends newsletters to its supporting members before opening nights. For example, in the newsletter for the original 1961 production of *The Crucible,* there are a number of background articles explaining America's past and present crises, that is, the witch trials and the anti-Communist investigations of the 1950s, and the relation between the two; there are also a number of what may be called foreground articles about the present social and political problems in Japan, including the controversial renewal of the Joint Security Treaty with America, known in Japan as *Anpo,* which ignited virulent protests across Japan. The prospective audience was told that "Miller's warning must be taken as our own," and there are further articles on the assassination by a right-wing youth of Asanuma Inejiro, the head of the Socialist Party, and another on Japanese international exchange projects with Taiwan and

"Red China" under the United States–Japan Peace Treaty. And, especially in the early programs and newsletters, there are several essays that attempt to educate the audience, to prepare them for the experience of Miller's plays.

Miller's history in Japan has been largely formed by a group of artists working in the Theater Troupe of Mingei. His future, however, remains in the hands of younger practitioners: the first Japanese production of *Salesman* in the twenty-first century was produced by the theater group Mumeijuku, starring Nakadai Tatsuya, an actor who met with Miller and received his permission to perform the play. The production was directed by Hayashi Kiyoto in January 2001. It was billed not as a story about America but as the story of the distortions caused by rapid social change as seen through the family of a common man, a salesman, both Japanese and American.

NOTES

1. See Peter D. Arnott, *The Theatres of Japan* (Tokyo: Tuttle, 1969), 228.

2. Actually the present name, *mingei,* echoes the original name of the group in the 1947–50 period—"minshu geijutsu gekijo," which is quite literally "the people's art theater."

3. Other companies producing Miller plays include the Subaru (Pleiades) Theater Group and the Haiyuza Actors' Theater.

4. Kurahashi Ken also translated Miller's autobiography, *Timebends,* and his book *Salesman in Beijing.*

5. The Supreme Commander for the Allied Powers was in effect in charge of occupied Japan, and this power was and is generally known in Japan as GHQ, general headquarters.

6. This is probably what Miller meant to say in *Salesman in Beijing,* when he wrote that that there were no "salesmen" in China.

7. There have been and probably still are men and women in the Japanese tradition who perform similar functions: telling the future, communicating with the dead, and casting spells. But here I am referring to the image of witchcraft in the West as an inverted form of Christianity.

8. Miller concludes that he would like the production to take place in theatrical space rather than in any specific locale. Miller returned to this issue in his play *Broken Glass,* in which one character states that there are Chinese Jews who might regard European Jews as un-Jewish.

9. Arthur Miller, *Salesman in Beijing* (New York: Viking, 1984), 72.

10. Arnott, *The Theatres of Japan,* 228.

11. Arnott, *The Theatres of Japan,* 259.

12. Miyagishi Yasuji, "Blank Pages for Those Left Behind," *Teatro,* October 23, 1975, 22.

Antonio R. Celada

The Reception of Miller's Theater in Spain

When Arthur Miller's plays reached Spain in the early 1950s, the Spanish literary scene was still deeply undermined by the effects of the Spanish civil war. The misery and poverty that beset Spain during a long period after the war and the isolation in which it found itself proved to be a great handicap to the survival of the revolutionary theatrical forms introduced in the late 1920s by Valle Inclán and García Lorca. Inclán, Lorca, and Miguel de Unamuno all died in 1936, and Max Aub, Rafael Alberti, and Pedro Salinas went into exile, leaving the Spanish stage practically devoid of talent. Experimental theater, socially committed theater, and modern productions with new settings were seriously restrained for economic reasons. Both commercial and stage-subsidized theaters turned to the so-called escapist comedies *(teatro evasivo)* to satisfy a public that was still traumatized by the horrors of war. Audiences were largely made up of spectators from the upper classes, since the prices charged for tickets were too expensive for the rest of the population. Thus, at the time, social injustice, exploitation, physical deprivation, or inhuman living conditions did not figure as suitable subject matter for theatrical representation; and the existence of a critical position toward the system or even the slightest questioning of authority was unheard of. Inevitably, the theater was exploited by the regime as a channel for propaganda, which painted a false picture of an untroubled and happy Spain.

Within this atmosphere one would think that socially committed foreign playwrights had very little to say to Spanish audiences. But that was not the case. American playwrights, especially Tennessee Williams and Arthur Miller, enjoyed remarkable success during the 1950s and 1960s. They both sent a breath of fresh air into the stalls of Spanish theaters where vision was, otherwise, extremely conservative. They also offered a new and original way to comprehend the human condition and the relationships formed among different groups. Their innovative style deliberately moved away from convention, and their characters were made of flesh and blood. They depicted ordinary people with problems typical of their class, which is why audiences could understand their situations easily. In general, the reception of American theater in Spain has been remarkable, and if we refer specifically to Arthur Miller, some of his plays were received with the greatest enthusiasm.

After the signing of the Madrid Agreement (1953), the United States and Spain enjoyed excellent political and social relations and, as a consequence, the ruling classes fostered American influence on various levels of Spanish culture. In many cases, the censorship characteristic of the dictatorship in the 1950s and 1960s showed much greater tolerance toward theater imported from the United States than it did toward its European counterparts and to its own national playwrights. The censorship imposed on Spanish theater was extremely severe, as reflected by the frequent cuts in scripts, occasional cancellations, manipulated translations, and adulterated versions: during the 1940s, for example, documents can be traced that show that about 10 percent of proposed productions were turned down and about 25 percent of those accepted were seriously mutilated.

The favorable political climate of mutual understanding that existed between the United States and Spain after the signing of the 1953 treaty generated a feeling of cordiality toward everything American. For at least three decades, Broadway held an irresistible attraction for Spanish theater, which considered it to be a symbol of modernity, prosperity, and progress. From its founding in 1957, *Primer Acto*, the Spanish magazine devoted to theatrical art, published articles, reviews, and news about American theater. And from the early 1950s to the late 1970s, the names that aroused most interest were Eugene O'Neill, Thornton Wilder, Tennessee Williams, Arthur Miller, and Edward Albee.

Miller was, without doubt, the most admired and successful American playwright to be performed in Spanish theaters in this period. His plays were seen throughout the country as a prominent testimony of the American way of life. Within Spanish theatrical circles, his work was considered to be a remarkable example of tradition and modernity combined. Spanish audiences were used to conventional and long-established dramatic devices and found Miller's traditional approach to certain subjects and conventions familiar. However, at the same time, they were receptive to new dramatic forms that they associated with the world of cinema, which they found particularly attractive.

From a social point of view, Miller boldly reflected upon and portrayed with great conviction both the tragedy and the drama of the urban common man. Spanish theatergoers were fascinated by characters such as Willy, a product of an unjust and inhumane system where there was no room for the weak. The most conservative sympathized with such a harsh critique because it confirmed the idea that no society could be just and prosperous if it forgot spiritual values. The most liberal also sympathized with Miller's message because in their view the theater should be a slice of life, presenting life as it really is and not as some people think it should be according to particular religious and moral norms. Few audience members, however, saw it as a threat to their ethical values, and they argued that their harmonious social relations, based on solid moral and spiritual needs, could hardly be undermined by the conduct of a materialistic society, lacking in faith. From this moment onward, moreover, all sides would see Miller's theater as the best mirror in which the virtues and defects of American society were reflected.

From a technical point of view, in terms of staging and setting, Miller was welcomed by those involved in the practical craft of theater. In his plays, they found both challenge and convention, boldness and caution, daring technical experiment and poetic dialogues. Spanish critics acknowledged his extraordinary success when applying new dramatic techniques such as flashbacks and the use of special lighting effects to stage multiple scenes on a single set. The lighting, music, empty space, and different levels for the presentation of simultaneous scenes all generated a sense of mutation of old forms and conventions. All of these innovations were appreciated by the most demanding audiences, not only those who regularly attended performances in Madrid and Barcelona, but especially by the younger generation who saw his plays at university or nonprofessional theaters.

This welcome combination of effects was perhaps the main cause of Miller's success in Spain. For very different reasons it was attractive to conservatives and liberals, to believers and agnostics, to people of all ages and to those professionally involved as theater practitioners. The tragedy of Willy Loman, Joe Keller, Eddie Carbone, and Maggie seemed to be far removed from Spanish cultural reality but not to the extent of being unfamiliar or unreasonable. There is, however, a group of great relevance without whose acceptance Miller's plays would not have become so popular in Spain: his fellow playwrights. Buero Vallejo on several occasions expressed his admiration for the creator of Willy Loman, as did Alfonso Sastre.

Critics and stage directors enthusiastically welcomed the work of Arthur Miller because it seemed to exemplify a long-awaited change taking place in theater in Spain. Literary circles of the 1950s and 1960s agreed almost unanimously that his drama represented a turning point, and most critics acknowledged that the successful staging in Madrid by José Tamayo of both *Death of a Salesman* in 1952 and *The Crucible* in 1956 marked a new beginning in Spanish theater. Tamayo established the Lope de Vega Company in 1946, the same year that Miller wrote *All My Sons*. With this project, he hoped to introduce radical changes into Spanish theater; his main objective was "to stage world famous plays but with a style that, really, represented a challenging response to Spanish theater of the time."[1] Among others, Miller's plays were soon to be produced in response to this idea.

Most of Miller's dramatic works were staged in Madrid and Barcelona, the two major centers of theater in Spain, before being produced in provincial capitals like Seville, Valencia, Santander, Pamplona, Oviedo, and Alicante. As might be expected, the level of acceptance by Spanish audiences was previously set by success obtained in Madrid and Barcelona. It is also important to note that foreign plays, Miller's especially, were usually staged by large companies who later toured the country. Strong actors, prestigious directors, and high-quality sets were progressively changing the experience of provincial theatergoers, who were generally far more conservative than audiences in the urban centers of Madrid and Barcelona.

All My Sons was the first play by Miller to be staged in Spain. It premiered on November 2, 1951, in the Teatro Comedia in Madrid, directed by José Gordon in a translation by Vicente Balart. It was staged by La Carátula, a *cámara* or chamber group, for a single performance. Cámara groups consisted of enthusiastic amateurs who were given a performance license for just one night, taking advantage of theater spaces left vacant when established companies took a day off. Due to this special arrangement and their more liberal audiences, they were in a strong position to incorporate into the Spanish repertoire foreign authors who would otherwise have had difficulties in the commercial theaters. They were also willing to stage works by young and as yet unknown Spanish playwrights. In addition, there was a clear political logic behind it: the new Spanish society after the civil war was to be preserved from foreign influence and its morals protected from supposedly decadent views. Under these circumstances, the repercussions the play had on Madrid audiences were minimal. Only a few reviews appeared, and they were mostly critical, taking note of the play's use of melodrama and lack of formal experimentation. *All My Sons* was more successfully staged in Madrid in 1963 at Teatro Recoletos, directed by Ricardo Lucía, who used the same version by Balart. On March 24, 1988, it was performed again with great success at Bellas Artes in Madrid, directed by Angel García Moreno in a new translation by Enrique Llovet. Augustín González, a well-known TV and movie star, played Joe Keller. Haro Tecglen in *El País* and Lorenzo López in *ABC* responded to the play as a vigorous and vibrant drama, emphasizing its energy as a well-made work in the Ibsen style, still fresh and relevant after forty years.

Death of a Salesman premiered on January 10, 1952, in the Teatro Comedia in Madrid and ran for 150 performances. It was directed by José Tamayo in the Spanish translation by José López Rubio. The original stage design by Sigfredo Burman was highly praised by reviewers and deftly conveyed the threat and claustrophobia that Willy complains about in the first act. Posters announcing the production not only contained the usual information about the cast, but also a message for Spanish audiences: "a sensational play, the winner of seven prizes in the United States! . . . As human as life itself." The last phrase was to divide critics for quite some time after the first night. While for some Willy was seen as a charming, sincere, cheerful—albeit contradictory—character, for others he was considered weak, cynical, materialistic, and unfaithful. If for some he represented the typical head of an American family defeated by an unfair system, for others he was the image of a man, destitute and forsaken, the result of a human being's abandoning spiritual values.

Although Miller was not yet well known by Spanish theatergoers in 1952, the success the play enjoyed on Broadway (742 performances) guaranteed resounding acclaim in Madrid. Audiences were similarly aware of the play's success in Buenos Aires in 1950 and in Caracas a year later. Enrique Ruiz has stated that the first performance of the play in Spain "represented an extraordinary event in the world of dramatic art; in theatrical terms it meant considerable innovation since to a certain extent its premiere implied a kind of earthquake."[2] Likewise, José Monleón explained that "North American theater conquered audiences here with *Death of a Salesman*."[3]

Miller's drama, however, was the cause of a considerable division among Spanish critics. The most striking case is the controversy between Alfonso Sastre and Torrente Ballester. In a piece published in *Arriba*, Ballester stated in a moralizing and pretentious tone that the play did not deserve the success that it had reaped because "the interest . . . is sociological, barely artistic and in no way poetic." Furthermore, "the play also fails from a technical point of view, for theatrical works of art are limited by space and time, and any attempt to break those boundaries will lead to chaos and confusion; it is an amorphous play . . . besides, it owes a great deal to the movies: more than theater can reasonably borrow, more than, by its very nature, can be permitted." Two days later in *Arriba* Sastre makes his point in an "Open Letter" in which he characterized Torrente's analysis as superficial, simplistic, and full of contradictions. Moreover, he continued, Torrente did not criticize the play, but the American way of life: "the drama is completely justified and successful . . . [and provides] a considerable amount of information." From Sastre's point of view, Torrente mixes sociological and artistic aspects; Willy's drama is perfectly conceived as authentic. Nothing in the play should be changed, but "what needs to be purified is the reality to which the drama testifies." Torrente expanded his views a few days later, speaking in general terms of ethics and aesthetics, tragedy and reality, and art versus propaganda.[4]

The impact of the Spanish premiere of *Salesman* was enormous, and the play was revived in a second Madrid production by Tamayo in 1959, this time at the Teatro Español. The reviews printed during the following days shared a common idea: though the production was not a premiere it might as well have been, since Willy Loman had not yet lost the freshness and vigor he had in 1952. The play returned to the stages of Madrid in 1985, on this occasion at the Bellas Artes, with the same director and in the same version, but with an additional attraction: Willy Loman was played by José Luis López Vásquez, a well-known actor from Spanish movies. The critical reviews were once more full of praise.

In December 2000 the Compañia del Centro Dramático Nacional presented a new *Salesman* directed by Pérez de la Fuente at the Teatro Principal in Barcelona. The production traveled to Madrid, Pamplona, Alicante, Seville, and Santander. At the playwright's request, the 1952 version by López Rubio was used. Willy Loman was played by José Sacristan, a much acclaimed Spanish movie actor who also played the role of Phillip Gellburg in *Broken Glass* in 1995. The production was a resounding success; newspapers, television, and, above all, the Internet, gave it such wide coverage that it became clear that Willy Loman had achieved an almost mythical status and could no longer be considered exclusively American; he now belonged to a universal cultural heritage and, as such, he remains a necessary reference in the national Spanish theater.

After the triumph of *Salesman*, Miller's new work was anxiously awaited in Spain. With Tamayo at the helm once again, *The Crucible* was staged by the Lope de Vega Company on December 20, 1956, at the Teatro Español in Madrid. The translation was by Diego Hurtado who, oddly enough, used the title chosen by Marcel Aymé for the French version: *Le sorcières de Salem* (in Spanish, *Las brujas de Salem*). If, as Hurtado noted, *The Crucible* could be translated into Spanish as *El Caldero* ("The Bucket"),[5] it is just as well that he decided to reproduce the French titles. *Las brujas de Salem (The Witches of Salem)* was the title by which the play was to be known in Spain until the release of the Twentieth Century Fox film in 1996, when it was translated more appropriately as *El Crisol*.

The same company, Lope de Vega, offered a new production of *The Crucible* in Barcelona in January 1957 at the Teatro Comedia before the run of the same play ended in Madrid. The new production was directed by Jose Luis Alonso and featured a different cast of actors, among whom Nuria Espert in the role of Abigail was highly praised. In Barcelona this production ran for almost 100 performances. Critics reacted favorably, describing the drama as profound and disturbing, a tragedy with characters of flesh and blood.[6]

In the critical reviews published immediately after the two premieres, however, there were no allusions to the McCarthy witch hunt. This was probably due to the self-censorship of journalists who did not want to risk a confrontation with the censors. Moreover, the elimination of political allusion by the translator contributed to this even further. But in later articles and reviews this topic was dealt with in depth, particularly in *Primer Acto*, which devoted three extensive articles to the issue of McCarthyism in the United States.[7] *The Crucible*, moreover, had a great impact on Spanish playwrights, who acknowledged the ease with which Miller dealt with delicate historical facts that could easily be recognized as a reference point for a contemporary political crisis.

The play received additional attention when Twentieth Century Fox released the film version in 1996; most reviews referred to the McCarthy period as one of the darkest in American history. The movie was a box office hit in Spain, and Miller's drama was received as a masterpiece of the stage and a metaphor for McCarthyite persecution. So great was the interest and the expectation surrounding the film that Tusquets published a translation of both the play and the movie script in 1997 with the titles *Las brujas de Salem* (drama) and *El Crisol* (script).

Another political play, *A View from the Bridge*, was performed in the Lara Theater in Madrid on September 19, 1958. It was directed by Pedro López Lagar who also played the role of Eddie in the translation by José López Rubio. Almost 150 performances were given over a period of four months. In February 1959 the play had its premiere in Barcelona, where nearly one hundred performances were given during a two-month run at the Teatro Comedia. *A View from the Bridge* was restaged in December 2000 in Valladolid, followed by a tour of several cities in the north of

Spain. The tour ended with resounding success in Madrid. The translation was by Eduardo Mendoza and the direction by Miguel Narros, one of the leading stage directors in Spain. Wide coverage in newspapers, magazines, and on the Internet responded to the social reality of contemporary Spain at the turn of the century: a world of immigration and of "people without documents." Spain has changed dramatically from the time of the play's premiere in 1958; *A View from the Bridge* now spoke to audiences with both immediacy and clarity.

By the time *After the Fall* was staged in the Teatro Goya in Madrid on January 11, 1965, Miller was a highly respected author in Spain. *Primer Acto*, which by that time had become the main scholarly journal on Spanish theater, dedicated a special issue to the play that included the translation.[8] Spanish audiences knew about Miller's relationship with Marilyn Monroe, the failure of their marriage, their divorce, and the movie star's suicide, and in the Madrid production Marisa de Leza (Maggie) looked remarkably like Monroe. In *Primer Acto* Fernando Santos questioned whether audiences in Madrid were going to the theater in order to be instructed in the philosophical matters supposedly present in the drama or whether, as he suggests, they were going out of morbid curiosity for a confession about the personal relationship between two public figures, one of whom died in tragic circumstances. Other contributors praised the play as "a philosophical social drama."[9] The play was directed by Adolfo Marsillach, who also played the role of Quentin. The version in Spanish was by José Méndez Herrera.

The Price had its opening night in the Teatro Figaro in Madrid on February 12, 1970, in a translation by José Méndez Herrera directed by Narciso Ibáñez Menta, who also took the role of Gregory Solomon. The brothers Victor and Walter were played by two well-regarded actors on the Madrid stage, Fernando Delgado and Jesús Puente. *After the Fall* was still very much in the audience's mind, and reviewers tried to underline what both plays had in common: confession as a means of redemption, the solitude of the individual's conscience, failure, frustration, but above all Miller's realistic technique in both situation and language.

From 1970 until 1995, the year in which *Broken Glass* was first staged in Madrid, Miller's work appeared with less frequency on the Spanish stage, but when *Timebends* was published in 1987 the critics and journalists paid attention to the author once more. The book was translated into Spanish and published in 1988 by Tusquets in Barcelona and sold well. On his way to Munich, Miller spent a few days in Madrid to present his autobiography to the press. Three of the most important newspapers at that time, *El País, ABC,* and *Diario* 16, published lengthy reports on both the publication of the book and the press conference. *Primer Acto* also covered Miller's presence in Spain.[10] Oddly enough, not much was said about the theater: most of the reporters centered their attention on those parts of the book that dealt with Miller's relationship with Monroe and his confrontation with the House Committee on Un-American Activities. Alfonso Sastre, the playwright who had been one of Miller's admirers, entitled the article he wrote for *Diario* 16 "Arthur Miller: An Author on the Decline?" thus giving the impression that an era in which theater from abroad had had considerable influence in Spain had come to an end. Miller's position as a reference point had slipped since the success of *The Price* in 1970. Indeed, by the year 2000 none of his later plays, with the exception of *Broken Glass,* had been performed in Madrid.

Broken Glass in a translation by Rafael Pérez Sierra opened at the María Guerrero in Madrid on April 7, 1995, and once again articles about Miller circulated in the news. The translation of his novel, *Focus,* was published the same year. Two key figures in the Spanish movie industry were involved in the premiere of the play: Pilar Miró, the director, and José Sacristan, who played the main character, Gellburg. The back cover of the program included a message from Miller himself; he apologized for not being able to attend the opening night and wished the actors every success. He also mentioned how much he admired "the tremendous talent of Spanish actors."[11]

Theater critics enthusiastically welcomed this new Miller, yet they could not help comparing it to the work of the late 1950s. In all of the reviews there is a reference to *Salesman;* and each review emphasizes the fact that although the action is weak in *Broken Glass,* the power of the dialogue is still intact. They also call our attention to Miller's exposure of anti-Semitism as something new in his drama (*Incident at Vichy,* it should be noted, has never been presented in Spain). It is also interesting to note how often the reviews mention the fact that Miller was by then eighty years old, seeming to imply that *Broken Glass* might be the last of his plays to be produced in Spain.

In the last decade of his life Miller visited Spain twice. In July 1997 he came to promote his novella, published in the United Kingdom as *A Plain Girl,* and to give a lecture in a summer course in El Escorial near Madrid, where he spoke about the theater. Once again he was in the press and on TV, and he focused on the problems that worried him: the theater no longer had the power of the old days; Broadway had nothing to say to the world; modern societies, which are materialistic and mechanized, are not easily seduced by the theater; its capacity for transmitting a message has been reduced considerably. Most national papers reported his concerns. But the most convincing evidence that Miller and his theater are still highly appreciated in Spain was the Premio Príncipe de Asturias de las Letras awarded to the playwright in 2002. In his letter to the Spanish consul in New York in which he expressed his gratitude for so great an honor and promised to come to Spain to receive it, he said: "I am fully aware of the international prestige of this award . . . I am especially pleased that this prize should come from Spain, a country in which my plays have always been greatly admired." Miller was in Spain during the last two weeks of October 2002; he received the prize in Oviedo, where, for the first time, he met Woody Allen, who also received the same award. The sixteen-member jury cited Miller as "the indisputable master of contemporary dramatic art," and said that his work captures "the concerns and conflicts of present-day societies"; he deserved the award because of "the constant humanistic revelation of his work which is characteristic of the best theater." In his speech at the ceremony on October 25 in Oviedo, Prince Felipe of Spain did justice to the importance of Miller's work and his contribution to the Spanish stage with the following words:

> Twentieth century theater cannot be understood without taking into account the work of this exceptional playwright . . . his amazing ability to interpret the society of his time and of all times, and to provide us, with defiance and a tremendous sense of justice, a source of constant reflection which suggests illuminating solutions. Arthur Miller has left an indelible mark on several generations of Spanish audiences, who, especially during the most difficult years, discovered intellectual stimulus and insightful moral orientation in his theater.[12]

NOTES

1. See Enrique Ruiz in 25 *años de Teatro en España* (Planeta, 1971), 6.
2. Ruiz, 25 *años de Teatro en España,* 6.
3. See José Monleón, *Primer Acto* 11 (November–December 1959): 43.
4. See Torrente Ballester, *Arriba,* January 15, 1952, 12. For additional responses, see *Arriba* on January 18, 1952, 6, and on January 20, 1952, 17.

5. See Diego Hurtado, *Informaciónes,* December 20, 1956, 7.

6. See *La Vanguardia,* January 8, 1957, 20.

7. See *Primer Acto* 2 (May 1957).

8. *Primer Acto* 61 (May 1965).

9. *Primer Acto* 61 (May 1965), 11.

10. See *El País Semanal* 598 (September 25, 1988): 28–42 and 599 (October 3, 1988): 54–60; *ABC,* December 20, 1988, 52–53; and *Diario 16,* December 6, 1988, 1–8 and December 21, 39–40. See also *Primer Acto* 226 (November–December 1988): 78–79.

11. Arthur Miller, program notes for playbill of *Broken Glass,* María Guerrero, Madrid.

12. Prince Felipe's speech, as well as the jury statement and the playwright's response, were given on the occasion of this award in Oviedo, Spain, on October 25, 2002.

Laura Cerrato

Arthur Miller in Buenos Aires

To speak of the fortunes of Arthur Miller in Buenos Aires implies a brief survey of the history of the theater and of the city. To what extent have Miller's plays and their reception by the press accompanied and unwittingly reflected the irregular developments of Argentine culture? Miller's theater covers approximately the second half of the twentieth century. The staging of his works is closely involved with the political events in Argentina and the history of mid-European migration, as well as the rise and establishment of a growing national theater.

His first play to be staged in Buenos Aires in Spanish, in the translation by Manuel Barberá, was *Death of a Salesman* in 1950. And I say in Spanish, because in the previous year a Yiddish version was staged. Few records of this 1949 premiere can be found in Argentine newspapers, except for its being mentioned in two reviews of the Spanish version the following year. One of them speaks of a "superb" Yiddish version, while the other says it was very inferior to the Spanish one. Good coverage of the production, however, appeared in a Jewish paper in Spanish, *Mundo israelita* ("Israelite World") on June 4, 1949, with a piece written by W. G. Gitrik about the director, Joseph Buloff, and the tragedy of Willy Loman. Gitrik emphasizes the importance of the play and the experience of Buloff, who had been working with the actors in Buenos Aires for two months. He also stressed that in New York the play was performed before sold-out audiences and was considered by critics to be the best American play of the past fifteen years. In spite of the fact that Buloff said he lost money every time his work was presented in Buenos Aires, he continued to do so because of his great wish to act in Yiddish, which apparently was becoming more difficult to do in the United States.

This point is very significant because it illustrates the role of immigrant communities in the development of drama in Buenos Aires. A playwright of Jewish origin found in Buenos Aires a city of cosmopolitan composition at that moment, a unique possibility of intercontinental crossings in a country still marked by xenophobia and anti-Semitism. New York was necessary for Miller as a site in which to find a universal language, one that would allow him to question, from a Jewish perspective, situations and aberrations that were also taking place in Buenos Aires and that would reappear even more dramatically in years to come. And Buenos Aires was necessary to Buloff so that he could, through a transplanted and translated Miller, preserve his own linguistic tradition, which allowed him to continue his work in English as well.

The reception of the Yiddish *Death of a Salesman* by the reviewers emphasized its similarities to Greek tragedy, at the same time recognizing its subject as essentially American and modern, one that is represented in Loman's loss of ideals and the discovery of the emptiness of an existence based on the Dale Carnegie bible. Great stress was given to the fact that the play is not subversive and deals mostly with a personal tragedy, avoiding propaganda, which perhaps indicates a note of caution related to the difficult times Argentina was going through under the first presidency of General Perón.

Another article by the same S. G. Gitrik appeared in *Mundo israelita* after the premiere and is an enthusiastic panegyric to the author and his creation of his extraordinary character, Willy Loman, and to the director and main actor, Joseph Buloff. The staging and performance of the rest of the company are, however, not mentioned. The style of both articles is both pompous and grandiloquent, discussing exclusively the message and overlooking any formal aspects of the staging. Lidia Goldman and Sonia Schalom, two actresses of the period, reported that Miller said Buloff's had been the best Willy Loman he had ever seen.[1]

Spanish-speaking theatergoers in Buenos Aires were introduced to Miller's theater in the 1950s; this decade was also marked by the end of the first presidency of the dictator Perón and great pressures on leftist manifestations, a very perceptible anti-Semitism, and an active hatred of North American imperialism. Drama and cinema were still severely controlled by censorship. The production of *Death of a Salesman* should be seen in this political context, rather than, for example, a staging of *All My Sons,* which was by this time known in book form but, with its allusions to corrupt profiteers, was a risky enterprise at this moment in the country's history.

It is important to note here that *All My Sons* had been premiered in 1947 in Bahía Blanca, an agricultural provincial town, apparently a national premiere. According to Carlos Foz, this event took place at the Anarchist Circle on May 1, performed by the organization's Philodramatic Group.[2]

During the two performances offered, a revolutionary text, *Bandera Negra* ("Black Flag"), was also read, a fact that helps place Miller's play within the context of an ideological struggle against reactionary forces, as they were seen at the time. It also explains to a certain extent the postponement of *All My Sons* in Buenos Aires, which had to wait for a more suitable moment from a political point of view.

The reception of the Spanish version of *Death of a Salesman* in 1950 was marked by great success, mostly as a result of two elements: the subject and the expressionist staging. While Willy Loman was seen as a representative of the middle class, his failure is nonetheless a universal one. Unlike the Yiddish articles about Buloff's version, in most reviews of the Spanish version Loman was seen as the typical victim of the capitalist system, more of a symbol than an individual with his own mistakes and misjudgments. These reviews refer to the oppression of contemporary man by unknown and brutal forces, with an arbitrary control over destiny. Some reviews stressed the dreamy nature of Loman, his lack of practical sense or adjustment to reality. Only one or two marked the fallacy of his values and idols. At this point Buenos Aires was also dreaming of easy success, unwilling to acknowledge the potential for economic and political disasters. Loman's reactions seemed normal—none of it was his fault and the system was always to blame. There is a confluence between the leftist intelligentsia and the fundamental anti-Americanism of the nationalistic parties *(peronistas* and *conservadores)* in detecting a common enemy in the American way of life, responsible for all of Loman's misfortunes. But we also find some allusions to a conspiracy of powers against Loman that might be read as veiled references to Perón's dictatorship.[3] Most reviewers stressed the nonlinear effect produced by the play's time shifts, though they were by no means unanimous in praising the way this production responded to this element in Miller's text. The Yiddish actor Buloff had, the previous year, efficiently used a simpler system of very brief blackouts. The Spanish *Salesman* could never quite account for this in formal stage terms.

In spite of the previously mentioned hesitation to stage *All My Sons,* the IFT group (Idischer Folks Teater), under the direction of David Licht, dared to do so as early as 1951. The play was presented in Yiddish, a very meaningful device of employing the language of a minority to introduce plays that in Spanish would have caused problems with censorship. This first adventure with Miller's polemic play was followed by versions in Spanish in 1954 (directed by Jack Denker) and in 1955 (by director Adrían Rey).

The premiere of *The Crucible* followed the same pattern. A Yiddish version was the first to introduce the play to Argentina. This time it was directed by a Bulgarian, Isidor Herschkovich, and a group called the Israelite Dramatic Art Company at the Teatro Astral in a collective translation. The different name of the company and their moving to another theater, not the IFT, was due to a combination of factors. The IFT had been closed down by the Argentine government in 1954 and 1955, so it was forced, with a changed name, to stage productions in borrowed venues. Opposing internal political currents within the Jewish community (Stalinists versus Zionists) caused a ban on IFT advertisements in the two Jewish newspapers in Buenos Aires, and the premiere of *The Crucible* passed unreviewed by the Yiddish press. The Spanish language press, on the other hand, acknowledged the production with brief descriptive reviews without any reference to the work's political implications. The Spanish newspaper *Clarín* referred to it as rural drama.

In July 1955, the Belgian National Theatre arrived in Buenos Aires with the French version of *The Crucible, La Chasse aux sorcières*. This event was more extensively covered by *La Nación, Clarín,* and *Diario El Mundo* (*La Prensa* had been closed down by the government). It is nevertheless typical of this Perónist period of censorship and repression that all the reviewers agreed to stress the historical and picturesque effects of the play, thereby avoiding other implications. A month later (August 1955), the Spanish version of *The Crucible,* directed by Marcelo Lavalle at the Instituto de Arte Moderno, was staged. *La Nación* stressed that in one month three versions of the play, in different languages, had been staged, but without venturing any interpretation of the fact, except to note the play's excellence and universal significance, avoiding any mention of political allegory. The scarcity of reviews during the period (and of these plays) is the result of both the comparatively little notice taken of these independent groups by the main newspapers, which were usually involved with commercial stagings of a much more frivolous nature, and the polemic contents of *All My Sons* and *The Crucible* that might have irritated local authorities.

But some underground magazines tried to make up for this lack of information in the main newspapers; these magazines included *La gaceta literaria, Fila O, La mascara, Teatro Libre de Buenos Aires,* and the Yiddish *Nai Teater.* In February 1956 *La gaceta literaria* published an article by Carlos Creste that was an evaluation of the importance of Arthur Miller's work and its relevance to the Argentine reader and audience. *Death of a Salesman, All My Sons,* and *The Crucible* were considered in their ideological context. In the three plays, Creste notes, the protagonist is the common man. "Individual, compact, familiar. None of them could become a revolutionary through a rational process. They are involved with the dominant régime, or else they believe in the pleasant myths of their times. . . . Suddenly, they are touched by infamy, humiliation, and destruction . . . a hero is then born, naturally, in spite of [himself]." After a brief analysis of themes and ideas in these plays, Creste sums up the virtue of Miller's theater:

> We must consider that Arthur Miller is a playwright in the cul-
> minating phase [of American theater]. He works upon very well
> defined antecedents: genre literature, unrooting . . . disappoint-
> ment, the application of expressionism to U.S. drama, and the
> cyclopic research summarized in the name Eugene O'Neill. . . .
> All the elements were already given; he confined himself to
> [employing] them, with a clear sense, oriented towards the
> importance of the essential, neatly, with sobriety. He doesn't
> show the aspirations of a renovator because he is a definite
> shaper. . . . He is the concisest playwright of his time.[4]

Printed next to this article and unsigned, although perhaps by the same writer, there appeared a short review of the three versions of *The Crucible* recently staged, emphasizing their significance and the enthusiastic reception. In June 1956, *La gaceta literaria* published a longer article by Bernardo Verbitzky, a distinguished journalist and essayist who later wrote a book on Arthur Miller,[5] analyzing the importance of his Argentine reception. Verbitzky's article was accompanied by excerpts from *A Memory of Two Mondays* and *A View from the Bridge,* recently staged by Pedro López Lagar. But it was not until 1963, when López Lagar restaged *A View from the Bridge,* that he was able to portray individual conflicts as something more than melodramatic. The treatment of individual passions and the role of the lawyer as a Brechtian spokesman, or chorus, previously considered melodramatic, was now praised by many critics; and the scenography by Saulo Benavente was highlighted for its ingenuity and inventiveness in dealing with the cinematographic structure. Such a radical shift in appreciation points to several cultural changes that were taking place at that moment:

1. Critics had become more sensitive to aspects that were not merely the
   plot or the actors' performances, taking the play as a complex phenomenon composed of different essential elements.

2. There was a withdrawal from the obsession with political messages, which had been quite natural after years of political censorship; this obsession was at this time giving way to aesthetic and psychological readings typical of the sixties.

The annus mirabilis for Arthur Miller in Buenos Aires was 1965. No less than five of his plays were staged: *The Crucible, All My Sons, A Memory of Two Mondays, After the Fall,* and *Death of a Salesman.* The Crucible was done by Marcelo Lavalle, who had premiered it ten years before, at the Instituto de Arte Moderno, one of the pillars of the independent theatrical movement. All the reviews agreed on the importance of this event, deploring the fact that it had not been staged for ten years. The great success of the play was due to two factors. One was the novelty of the subject, with overtones of medieval events in a Puritanical context, both elements still exotic in Argentina. But more importantly, the audience was now quick to appreciate the subtext of the play, with its references to persecution, ideological fanaticism, and intolerance. This was an idiom easily understood by different layers of society in Argentina.

One month later, Buenos Aires's theatergoers could see a version of *All My Sons* staged in Yiddish by the Jewish Warsaw State Theater, which also toured it in the main provincial capitals. This time Spanish-speaking papers such as *Clarín* and *La Prensa* devoted important reviews to this foreign performance. Both considered that the play had not aged well. *La Prensa* found it slow and oppressive, but praised the actors, who gave it moments of authentic dramatic intensity. In *Clarín,* Edmundo Guibourg wrote an odd review that started by stating that it wasn't a good idea for the Polish Theater to try to renew their traditional and popular repertory with a play by Miller, because it was one of his early plays and still full of melodramatic effects. He also objected to the generalized tendency of critics to connect this play with Henrik Ibsen. He allowed a certain affinity with *An Enemy of the People* (staged in Buenos Aires in 1961) but found Miller's play more melodramatic and, therefore, démodé. Nevertheless, he admitted that this play anticipated fundamental subjects and attitudes in Miller's later works, such as the psychology of the anti-hero, the unmasking of superstitions and lies, the alternatively violent and sentimental relationship between parents and children, and, above all, the implacable expiation brought about not by an illusory final judgment but by the judgment of men.

These observations from 1965 contrast tellingly with the reception of the same play in 1984 and especially in 1988. What in the sixties was seen as démodé, truculent, and melodramatic, lacking in experimental concerns and boringly realistic, twenty years later was hailed as a courageous denunciation of decadence and corruption, reflecting the changes that had taken place in Argentina between those periods.

Buenos Aires, in 1956, had plunged into the world of the avant-garde and experimentalism, mostly due to the influence of dramatic innovations brought about by the Instituto Di Tella, leader of the new theater, which sponsored research and experimentalism in collective creations, happenings, the death of the author, and the theater of the absurd. On the other hand, the Argentine society that came back to life after the military dictatorship of 1976–1984 was thirsty for ethics and ideological tolerance. And in 1988, there was already disappointment in the recently acquired democracy, so much so that the audience and critics displayed an extreme sensitivity to any sign of corruption from those in power.

A Memory of Two Mondays, also staged in the landmark year of 1965, is in general considered a minor play, and it was considered as such at the time. The premiere of *After the Fall* in August produced a much more provocative set of reviews. This was partly due to the cast, including very important actors of the time, and the director, the Brazilian Flavio Rangel, but even more so by the biographical and confessional features of the play. As in New York, reviewers objected to its impudent exhibitionism, sensationalism, and exposure of Miller's former wife, Marilyn Monroe. Very little was said about the staging, but a great deal about the supposed moral transgression in Quentin's reprehensible relationship to women, especially by *La Nación,* the most important morning paper, which had a very pronounced Catholic ideology. The popular *Clarín* and the liberal *La Prensa* preferred to concentrate on the play's dramatic and psychological aspects. This more sympathetic attitude contrasted the play with *Death of a Salesman; After the Fall* was considered much more daring because of its more fluid use of conventional space and time patterns. It was also more difficult to stage. It is revealing to note how these two attitudes toward the play marked a gap that would soon develop between Argentina's Catholic, conservative intellectuals and the country's liberal thinkers. This would be confirmed by the coup of General Onganía in the following year (1966), establishing a dictatorship extremely intolerant on the subject of morality and private life. Its consequences, in the long run, would be the third presidency of General Perón in 1974, supported by a guerilla war; this in turn would lead to a reaction causing another military coup in 1976 with its ugly sequel of missing and tortured people. This sequence of reactionary political attitudes may have started with these early traces of puritanical bigotry, apparent not only in the reactions to *After the Fall* but also in responses to plays belonging to the so-called tradition of the absurd. Such is the case of *El desatino* by Griselda Gambaro, termed by Francisco Mazza Leiva as pornographic because of the use of female nudity and four-letter words.[6]

The IFT had, since 1957 (once Perón's second presidency and the revolution that had overthrown him had ended), turned its back on Yiddish and shifted to Spanish for its performances. The theatergoers who could understand Yiddish were obviously diminishing and, besides, protection against censorship or anti-Semitism was no longer necessary. But it also ended the brilliant career of the group, which had started as far back as 1933. In September 1965, a version of *Death of a Salesman* was again staged, in Spanish, and directed this time by Oscar Ferrigno. Despite positive reviews, however, the old enthusiasm was gone. In Spanish, the IFT became one more of so many theaters. There was still something left of the old partisan attitude, though, in the fact that the translation used, by the same Manuel Barberá who had done it ten years before, had now been revised, substituting for the more refined Spanish second-person pronounced *tú* the Argentine *vos,* more colloquial and specific to the working classes at that moment.

In 1967 Die Deutsche Kammerspiele traveled to Buenos Aires to stage *After the Fall* in German, and a year later a Spanish translation of *The Price* was staged in Buenos Aires a few months after its world premiere in New York. The reaction to both productions was similar, revealing a sense of fatigue about social problem plays as well as a call for formal experimentalism rather than a reliance on profuse decor. The fact is that Miller's plays, which had started in the late forties as underground performances at an anarchist center, were beginning to turn into a typical product for calle Corrientes (equivalent, in its meaning, to Broadway), meant for an audience of a well-to-do middle class that loved to see itself as caring for the problems of less fortunate people, but refusing to take note of avant-garde, demanding, unorthodox, and experimental theater.

In this way, plays and playwrights who had been considered groundbreaking in previous decades were to be confined to a more conservative audience. In the seventies, other factors contributed to dividing the audience into separate camps (something like Broadway, off Broadway, and off-off Broadway), a phenomenon never seen before in Argentina. Among the issues here were ideological intolerance, a populist and leftist tendency during the presidency of Cámpora and Perón, and a marked right-wing fundamentalism during the last military dictatorship. On another level, the end of the seventies and beginning of the eighties witnessed the appearance of a new dramatic trend announcing the death of the playwright in favor of collective creation and a revival of Argentine writers who tried to rid themselves of foreign influences. All this led to a momentary banishment of the more traditional, well-made play. Nevertheless, from the seventies to the turn of the century Miller's plays in Buenos Aires were staged in response to the changing climate of political and social reality in Buenos Aires. In 1970 *Incident at Vichy* was produced for the first time and under very special circumstances. The increasing moral censorship had closed down the Odeón Theater because of the ban on Mart Crowley's *The Boys in the Band,* a landmark play consisting almost exclusively of male homosexual characters. Apparently, *Incident at Vichy* was the only work available that could employ the twelve actors engaged for Crowley's play. The production opened to mostly negative reviews—ironic in that a few years later anti-Semitism would resurface in a specifically Argentine context.

A new production of *A View from the Bridge* was staged in 1971 with the added attraction of being performed on an unused bridge over the Riachuelo River, increasing the realistic atmosphere of the play. A year later Ibsen's *An Enemy of the People* in Miller's adaptation was the cause of a long struggle with censorship, which was intent on cutting parts of the play that "would be all right to include in normal times, but would now be an obstacle to the institutionalizing process in which the country is engaged."[7] This was reported by the magazine *Siete Días* as having been said by a Secretary of Culture to Kive Staiff, director of the Teatro Municipal San Martín. *La Nación* described this struggle in detail. It apparently started when the official attended one of the rehearsals during which Roberto Durán, the director, used improvisational techniques to help each actor find the best wording for what he had to say, doing away with places and dates excessively circumscribed. Finally, the government partially had its own way: Miller's text would not be mutilated, but the interventions provided by director and actors would not be allowed. With this, the more direct allusions to contemporary political reality were circumvented, mirroring Miller's own perspective when adapting his version of Ibsen to the McCarthy context. Again, the reaction of the press was symptomatic of the times. Some, like the magazine *Siete Días* (in a review by Emilio A. Stevanovitc), preferred not to mention the incident, criticizing instead some of Miller's changes and quoting Jean-Paul Sartre's negative opinion of it. Others, like *La Nación,* reported the problem accurately but suggested that everything did not end well. *La Opinión* (openly in favor of the guerillas) and *Primera Plana* were alert to the dramatic irony of the situation. Francisco Urondo *(La Opinión)*, later killed by the next military government, famously described the entire episode as *"An enemy of the people* within the 'enemy of the people.'"

Between 1972 and 1976, during the last presidency of Perón, the model followed was a violent denial of any kind of foreign art, in favor of what the government called "national reality," which was even turned into a subject to be taught at school. The reaction, with the military coup of 1976, substituted this fundamentalism with another quite as crude, centered on the persecution of the left and all potential supporters of the guerrilla movement. In spite of this, or maybe because of it, several plays by Miller were restaged between 1976 and 1984: *The Crucible* in 1972, *A View from the Bridge* in 1976, *Death of a Salesman* in 1979, *The Crucible* in 1983, and *The Price* and *All My Sons* in 1984. In this period social readings of these plays were increasingly dominant. One of the main reasons for this was the politically minded atmosphere in general, whether under the rule of populist or demagogical regimes.

The next decade of Miller in Argentina saw the arrival of two plays with a different significance: *Broken Glass* and *A Memory of Two Mondays.* The premiere of *Broken Glass* in 1995 forced audiences to consider the reality of Nazism within the context of what the reviewer for *Clarín*, Gerardo Fernández, called a psychological thriller. Fernández noted that "broken glass" was a metaphor for many other disintegrations besides that of *Kristallnacht.* The play had somehow produced this evident division between critics who were altogether taken by its anti-anti-Semitism and those who dared to open the play up to consider additional meanings.

In 1996 a new version of *A Memory of Two Mondays,* directed by Agustín Alezzo, spoke to new audiences with alarming clarity. In *Clarín* Olga Cosentino drew parallels between the play and present conditions for the working classes. And, unfortunately, the point she made was entirely persuasive. A high rate of unemployment and inflation, a freeze in wages with an ever-increasing number of working hours for the same salary, students forced to work while they went to school, all leaped from Miller's play into everyday life, turning unnecessary any attempt to adapt the play to the present. The play was a final homage to the playwright's visionary powers—at least in terms of the vexed history of Miller and politics, as usual, in Argentina.

I wish to express my gratitude to Professor Ana María Cartolano for her help in collecting the archive material that has been used in this study.

NOTES

1. In conversation with the author. Miller saw Buloff's production in New York.

2. Carlos Foz is in charge of the Archive of Teatro San Martín in Buenos Aires. He has done important research on anarchist drama in Argentina. This information about the first staging of a play by Miller in my country was verified by him with the program of the event. See Carlos Foz, *Sistema educativo y teatral anarquista en la República Argentina* (Salamanca: Real Universidad de Salamanca, 1997). See also Teresa Najchaus, "IFT 1931–1982," in *Teatro IFT 50 Aniversario* (November 1982), 50. It should be noted that many records of IFT performances were destroyed in the bombing of the AMIA (Asociación Mutual Israelita Argentina) Center in Buenos Aires on July 18, 1994, in which eighty-five people died.

3. See Foz, *Sistema educativo y teatral anarquista en la República Argentina.*

4. Carlos Creste, "Arthur Miller en Buenos Aires," *La Gaceta Literaria* (February 1956).

5. Bernardo Verbitzky, *El teatro de Arthur Miller* (Buenos Aires: Siglo Veinte, 1960).

6. Francisco Mazza Leiva, review of *El desatino,* by Griselda Gambaro, *Hoy en la cultura,* December 1965.

7. Cited from *Siete Días* (1971).

Kirsten Herold

Miller in Scandinavia
Focus on Denmark

In his autobiography, *Timebends,* and again during a major interview held on the occasion of his eighty-fifth birthday, Arthur Miller laments that he has often had more recognition abroad than he has had in his own country.[1] He attributed this in part to the loss of a genuine theater culture in the United States and to the fact that European theater is still heavily subsidized. Denmark would certainly be a case in point. In the years since the first Danish production of *Death of a Salesman,* Miller's plays have been performed frequently—in the state-subsidized National Royal Theater in Copenhagen and in the three major regional theaters, Aarhus, Aalborg, and Odense, as well as in commercial venues. In other words, Miller's works have been critically acclaimed as modern classics, while also proving commercially viable. Indeed, after Henrik Ibsen and August Strindberg, there has been no playwright of comparable importance in the Danish theater.[2]

The numbers alone tell the story. In a country of five million people, Miller's plays are frequently performed, and in the past two decades more so than ever. *Salesman* alone has been given several professional productions, three of them mounted in the 1990s. During the 2000–2001 season, the most important theater in Denmark, the National Royal Theater, celebrated the fiftieth anniversary of the original Danish production of *Death of a Salesman* with a new staging of the landmark play. *The Crucible, All My Sons, A View from the Bridge, After the Fall, Incident at Vichy, The Price, The Ride Down Mt. Morgan,* and *Broken Glass* have all been seen in multiple productions during the same period. The film version of *Salesman* with Dustin Hoffman (originally made for American TV) had a long and successful run, as did the 1996 film version of *The Crucible,* and *Salesman* is one of the most frequently taught texts at the high school and college level, where it is traditionally interpreted as an indictment of the so-called American dream. Moreover, the Danish translation of the play can be found in many homes. In short, *Salesman* is the seminal text of post–World War II drama in Denmark.

Part of the reason for Miller's enormous impact can be seen as simply being in the right place at the right time. First produced in 1950, *Salesman* arrived on the Danish scene at a historical moment ready to welcome international and particularly American influences. At the same time, Miller's dramaturgy felt very familiar, as the play was performed in the tradition of the Ibsenite, socially realistic drama so well known to Scandinavian audiences. *Salesman* also came along when people could afford to go to the theater again. Denmark had been under German occupation from 1940 to 1945, and, although it had suffered nowhere near the hardships of many other European countries, the economy had been considerably depressed.

Most important, after a long draught, the late 1940s were particularly receptive to international drama. The theater of the 1930s had been both nationalistic and didactic (with the exception of Kjeld Abell), and during the war dramatic activity limited its scope even further. Actual resistance to the Germans was largely passive until 1943, but one way to register protest was to assert one's national identity in all the arts. Thus, the dramatic repertoire consisted largely of the Danish classical pieces of the eighteenth and nineteenth centuries (by writers such as Ludvig Holberg, Johan Ludvig Heiberg, and Adam Oehlenschlager), the Bournonville ballets, various musicals with historic themes, or escapist entertainment.[3] With the selection of films severely limited by the ban on British and American fare, theater was one of the few public arenas for the performing arts. After 1943, when the policy of cooperation broke down, the job of the censor (a Danish national who saw his main function as keeping Danish actors and directors out of German prisons) was made even more difficult because anything that hinted of nationalism was banned.[4] The situation reached a crisis in 1944 when the Germans kidnapped and brutally murdered the leading Danish playwright of the time, the minister Kaj Munk, author of several patriotic historical dramas.

After the war, domestic dramatists returned to Ibsenite problem plays, but at the same time the door was also open to plays from the international community. From the late 1940s on, the play list of the Copenhagen theaters included the most important names in modern and contemporary drama. The existentialist theater of Jean-Paul Sartre and Albert Camus, and especially Jean Anouilh, had a big audience in the late 1940s, as did the eagerly anticipated plays of Eugene O'Neill, whose *Iceman Cometh* (produced in 1948), *A Moon for the Misbegotten* (1956), and *Long Day's Journey Into Night* (1957) were all huge successes. The way was thus paved for the younger American dramatists, the so-called American neorealists, which is to say Miller and Tennessee Williams.[5]

The original 1950 production of *Death of a Salesman* played 112 times (a lot for Denmark) and was a triumph for Johannes Meyer, the popular actor in the main part. Whether it made grown men cry (as the New York production supposedly did) is doubtful, given the phlegmatic Danish temperament, but to the many people who saw it, it became one of those once-in-a-lifetime theater experiences, with spontaneous applause interrupting the emotional highlights. The reviews were uniformly rapturous: the set was praised for its suggestiveness (doors, windows, etc., were merely hinted at), so that the audience really felt as if it were inside a person's head. In other words, the play was not designed too realistically. The cast was viewed as nearly perfect; some reviewers had also seen the New York production and commented that Danes in supporting roles were even better than those in the United States. They also noted that the Danish version worked as an ensemble piece, not just a star vehicle.[6] Reviews explained the success of the *Salesman* with Danish audiences in the following way: although Danish society was not yet as competitive as the America of the play, after the lean years of the Depression and the German occupation, people could readily relate to the feeling of having worked all their lives and then being left with nothing. There was no question but that this was a modern classic.[7]

The audience quickly increased when *Salesman* was performed as a radio play, with the same cast, and broadcast to huge acclaim repeatedly throughout the 1950s (and even occasionally into the later decades, most recently in the early 1990s to commemorate the hundredth birthday of Johannes Meyer). Radio plays have traditionally been a very important genre in Denmark, where many aspiring playwrights have had their start. Indeed, in Denmark *All My Sons* and *The Crucible* have also had successful runs as radio plays.

Since its premiere there have been at least ten other productions of the play. In 1981 the play was produced by a commercial Copenhagen theater in a financially successful version, apparently by overplaying the sentimentality and treating Willy and Linda very sympathetically. Another commercial production, in 1990, took the opposite approach. With a new translation (critics complained that the idioms were too modern), this Willy was so "shrill, hollow, false, choleric, lyrical, and sentimental" that his two sons seemed to become his victims. Thus, his death was hardly tragic.[8]

The National Royal Theater produced a fiftieth anniversary production, performed on the same stage as the original, to mostly respectful reviews.[9] In general, in this production, as in the 1990 version, critics noted a shift of emphasis from the social-political issues to father-son relationships. One less enthusiastic critic complained that the production as directed by Vibeke Bjelke was too heavy-handed, a classic on a pedestal, and that the play needed cutting. One telling complaint was that this version was played too realistically. Jens Kistrup, Denmark's most respected drama reviewer, quoted a passage from *Timebends* in which Miller discusses the need for a new dramatic form that would dissolve the lines between past and present. This production, however, relied too much on conventional stage realism—even the scenes with Ben were played straight out, with no mystery or dreamlike quality.[10] Such emphasis on fourth-wall realism has been symptomatic of the Danish approach to Miller's work in general.

A commercial house in Copenhagen, the New Theater, received the rights to *The Crucible,* which opened in 1953 to a successful run. Denmark did not undergo any McCarthyism per se, but did experience a fair amount of anti-Communist hysteria all the same.[11] More recent productions of this play have focused primarily on the theme of sexual repression and the recurring need for scapegoating. Danes were accustomed to thinking about Americans as puritanical and sexually repressed, and events like the Monica Lewinsky affair or the more recent Mark Foley scandal seemed to support this caricature. *The Crucible* has seen more innovative productions than *Salesman* and has suffered less from the heavy-handed, overly realistic approach that has often marred *Salesman.*

The most memorable recent production of *The Crucible* was directed by the controversial director Henrik Sartou in 1994 at Folketeateret in Copenhagen. Sartou had acted in the play when he was in theater school and hated every minute of it. In Sartou's view, politics is a dead end, "something you talk about when you are not capable of talking about love and feelings." For Sartou the play was about repressed male desire, about male fear of "the other," women, and sexuality.[12] Although this interpretation was undeniably exciting, it was to one reviewer at least an oversimplification, because it reduced a complex set of interpersonal issues to a purely individual question. After all, the play retains its power because it is also about political hysteria, anywhere and anytime. With a "pompous staging," pounding music, and bizarre elements of clowning and juggling, the play became (literally) a black-and-white drama about right and wrong.[13]

Miller's late plays, *Broken Glass* and *The Ride Down Mt. Morgan* have both been produced in the 1990s.[14] *The Ride Down Mt. Morgan* opened at the Folketeateret on September 23, 1993.[15] The sole reviewer considered the play "soporific" and argued that one quickly came to envy the popular actor playing Lyman, Jesper Langberg, who spent most of the play in bed, "sighing like Winnie the Pooh." The director was unable to light a fire under the play, and there was nothing irresistible about Langberg, accused of being "a wet, heavy Danish wool sock."[16]

Broken Glass, which opened at the National Royal Theater March 15, 1997, received much more attention, albeit mixed. The opening of the play coincided with several highly publicized anti-Semitic incidents in Sweden and Denmark, in addition to the events in the Balkans, so the play was welcomed as topical, especially by critics. Yet in his headline, *Politiken's* reviewer, Brent Mohn, declared the play "very dull" and found Miller's linking of private and universal issues "distasteful." Other reviewers found the play, though conventional and heavy-handed, intensely provocative and exciting.[17] The veteran director, Vibeke Bjelke, who would go on to direct the fiftieth anniversary production of *Salesman,* called her production of *Broken Glass* one of her most rewarding experiences in the theater, and it was a big audience success. Of all the plays she has been involved with, this one gave her the most personal set of responses and the greatest number of letters from an appreciative audience: "after all, in Denmark it takes a lot before people sit down and write you a letter."[18]

In explaining Miller's appeal on the Danish stage, one cannot simply point to "the right place at the right time," although that is clearly part of the reason. Especially in the years following World War II, Danes experienced an almost universal love and gratitude toward Americans as liberators from the Germans. Yet, at the same time, most people were already beginning to experience more complicated feelings towards all things American, an ambivalent set of reactions that continues to this day. The societal problems of the United States, as Danes see them—the increasing gap between rich and poor, the concentration of economic power in fewer hands, the rise of vast chains and shopping malls, the destruction of cities, racial problems, rising crime, and an increasingly media-driven political climate—all these have been and are to this day seen as omens of things to come in Europe; in fact, they are already there. An American playwright like Miller, who is very much part of his culture yet stands in a critical relation to it, is extremely congenial to Danish interests and attitudes. Danes look to Miller and see a kindred spirit.

The other primary reason for Miller's prominence is the Danish love of realism with its formal theatrical conservatism. Although Denmark still has a genuine theatergoing culture, both in Copenhagen and in the smaller towns, one can easily argue that what is available continues to be rather narrow. In the Danish theater, realism with a social dimension and in the Ibsenite style, has long been the preferred mode of representation. Sociopolitically inflected realism, of course, can make for powerful theater, but one might indeed sense that this is not the only possible kind of drama. A recent lament, entitled "Did Nora Go Anywhere At All?" published in the leading cultural newspaper *Information,* points out that ever since 1879 (the year *A Doll's House* had its world premiere in Copenhagen), Danish audiences and critics have essentially wanted theater that they can understand and relate to, nothing more.[19] As late as 1999, it was considered both new and innovative when Michael Frayn's *Copenhagen* was performed in the round. Even in the case of Ibsen and Strindberg, the plays that have found audiences have consistently been the realistic plays—for Ibsen *A Doll's House, An Enemy of the People, Ghosts,* and *Hedda Gabler,* but certainly not the more experimental late plays. In Strindberg's case, the popular plays are *The Father, The Stronger,* and *Miss Julie,* not *A Dream Play* or *Ghost Sonata.* In this respect, the Danes have been more literal-minded than the Swedes, who have had strong interest in the late Strindberg. The epic theater of Bertolt Brecht is respected but has had little influence outside the political fringe. Of course, especially since the 1960s, there has been much alternative theater (in part because of generous state funding), but it too has found only a small coterie audience. Mainstream theater—the state-subsidized theaters, the commercial Copenhagen theaters, and radio and TV—has stayed firmly on the side of the traditional, realistic problem plays and seems likely to stay that way in the foreseeable future.[20] To many young actors and directors, the state of the Danish stage is, therefore, like an old lady "staggering along stiffly on her crutches."[21] Theater in Denmark has become synonymous with culture and even cultural heritage. People go to the theater because they ought to, because "goddamn it, it is Arthur Miller, it must be good."[22] Given that dubious set of circumstances, Miller's influence seems unlikely to diminish anytime soon.

NOTES

1. See Arthur Miller, *Timebends: A Life* (New York: Grove Press, 1987); and Enoch Brater, "A Conversation with Arthur Miller," in *Arthur Miller's America: Theater and Culture in a Century of Change,* ed. Enoch Brater (Ann Arbor: University of Michigan Press, 2005), 244–55.

2. For their help in researching the performance history of Miller in Denmark, I am indebted to Niels Krabbe, director of the Music and Drama Department at the Royal Library in Copenhagen, and his assistants; the staff at the University Library

in Aarhus; my sister, the actress Hanne Fogh Pedersen, who has performed in *The Crucible;* and the director Vibeke Bjelke, whose productions of *Broken Glass* and *Death of a Salesman* are discussed in this essay.

3. See Kela Kvam, et al., *Dansk Teaterhistorie* [Danish Theater History], vol. 2 (Copenhagen: Glydendal, 1992), 175–78.

4. Kvam, *Dansk Teaterhistorie,* 178–84.

5. Tennessee Williams's drama had already been presented in Denmark with *The Glass Menagerie* and *Summer and Smoke* at Riddersalen in 1948–49 and *A Streetcar Named Desire* at the Royal Theater in 1949. *Cat on a Hot Tin Roof* was a popular success at the New Theater in 1956.

6. See, for example, Harald Engberg, "En Saelgers Dom" [A Salesman's Dream], *Politiken,* March 16, 1950, 15–16.

7. Engberg, "En Saelgers Dom," 15–16.

8. See Paul Jorgen Budtz, *Ekstra Bladet,* January 17, 1990, sec. 1, 25; and Michael Bonnesen, "Willy Logneren" [Willy the Liar], *Politiken,* January 17, 1990, sec. 3, 2.

9. The first Danish production of *Salesman* was staged in 1950.

10. See Bettina Heltberg, "En dod Sild" [A Dead Herring; an untranslatable pun], *Politiken,* August 27, 2000, sec. 2, 3; and Jens Kistrup, "Om en mad der hed Loman" [About a Man Named Loman], *Weekendavisen,* August 27, 2000, sec. 2, 2.

11. Kvam, *Dansk Teaterhistorie,* 195.

12. See Peter Thygesen, "Henrik Sartou hadede Arthur Millers *Heksejagt*" [Henrik Sartou Hated Arthur Miller's *Witch Hunt*], *Politiken,* September 16, 1994, sec. 2, 3.

13. See Me Lund, "Mandefantasier i Morket" [Male Fantasies in the Dark], *Berlingske Tidende,* September 18, 1994; and Thygesen, "Henrik Sartou hadede Arthur Millers *Heksejagt,*" sec. 2, 3.

14. The Danish title *Broken Glass* is *Krystal,* a very good choice that has the advantage of alerting Danes to the horror of Kristallnacht.

15. *Farlige Forbindelser* (literally, "Dangerous Double Dealings," a far less interesting title than the original) is the Danish title for *The Ride Down Mt. Morgan.*

16. See Jonna Gade, *Ekstra Bladet,* October 1, 1993, sec. 1, 20.

17. See Bent Mohn, "Privat Lammelse: *Krystal* er et meget kedelight Miller stykke" [Private Paralysis: *Broken Glass* Is a Very Dull Miller Play], *Politiken,* March 15, 1997, sec. 2, 6; Annette Bjorg Koeller, "Uhyggelight aktuelle Miller" [Frighteningly Relevant Miller], *Berlingske Tidende,* March 13, 1997, sec. 2, 2; and Me Lung, "Samvittighed" [Conscience], *Berlinske Tidende,* March 15, 1997, sec. 2, 8.

18. Vibeke Bjelke in a telephone interview with the author, November 4, 2001.

19. Anne Middleboe Christensen, "Gik Nora Overhovedet Nogensteder?" [Did Nora Go Anywhere at All?], *Information,* December 28, 1999.

20. Christensen, "Gik Nora Overhovedet Nogensteder?"

21. Katrine Wiedemann and Jens Albinus, *Jyllands-Posten,* November 7, 2000, sec. Kunst og Kultur, 2.

22. Wiedemann and Albinus, *Jyllands-Posten,* 2.

Louis Marks

The Crucible
Three British Encounters

In *Timebends,* Arthur Miller recounts hearing with pleasure from George Devine, artistic director of the Royal Court Theatre, London, about the enthusiastic reception of his 1956 production of *The Crucible* by its "eager young audience."[1] I was in that audience and can bear witness to not only our enthusiasm for the play but the kind of messages we took from it. We saw it overwhelmingly as a coded onslaught on McCarthyism that, while not an active political menace in Britain, nevertheless engaged the emotions of all, as I saw it, right-thinking people in our generation. Earlier I had carried round petitions demanding clemency for the Rosenbergs and my own political credentials were plainly radical. But I was surely not alone that night at the Court in applauding Miller as a champion of sanity against the anticommunist hysteria we felt was gripping America and that might spill across the Atlantic.[2]

Shortly after this I was brought face-to-face with the realities of this modern day witch hunt when I was fortunate to be hired as a trainee script editor by a remarkable expatriate American film producer in London, Hannah Weinstein, who offered much-needed succor to blacklisted writers back home by hiring them to write under pseudonyms for popular television series. Thus I found myself working alongside such legendary talents as Ring Lardner, Jr., and Ian Hunter and learned much about the wonders of creativity that could arise from a sparky story conference in such company, as also about the tragedies that blighted the lives of those whose careers had been lopped off by the House Committee on Un-American Activities.

Lardner, like Miller, defied the committee, refusing to give names, but, unlike Miller, he served a year's imprisonment for his pains. Lardner survived. Others, many others, went under. *The Crucible* was almost a manifesto for those who resisted, and the moment that lingered longest in the mind was when the condemned Proctor in the last scene "with a cry of his soul" refused to put his name to the recantation. "Because it is my name! Because I cannot have another life!" he says. "Because I am not worth the dust on the feet of them that hang!"[3] And is led off to the gallows. McCarthyism was also about names.[4]

Time jump forward to 1980. A quarter of a century on and we are in a very different world. The sixties and seventies have relegated McCarthyism to the history books. Ideology of every sort is in retreat; except ironically in Britain where the last of the great ideological leaders of the twentieth century, Margaret Thatcher, had begun battering down the ramparts of established tradition in the name of the free market. One of our greatest cultural institutions, soon also to be in the firing line, was the British Broadcasting Corporation (BBC), where after some years of freelancing I had been invited to work in 1970, first as a script editor and from 1976 as a producer. Three years later I was asked to take charge of one of the corporation's three major and longest-standing drama strands, *Play of the Month*. And so the ground was prepared for my second encounter with Miller's masterpiece.

In the twenty-five years since the Royal Court production, *The Crucible* had clearly established itself as one of the major dramatic works of the century and an eminently suitable candidate for *Play of the Month,* whose brief was to offer viewers a chance to see on their screens in their own living rooms the finest of world theater from the Greeks to the present day. That sounds perhaps too earnestly Reithian and the phrase "museum piece" was often bandied about the office as a turnoff. My view was that if a play had become a museum piece it was either not a very good play to begin with or one that was missing the core of magic that made it work in its own day. Or, to put it another way, any truly great play should be able to work in any period, and audiences should be able to see in it truths that illuminate the present as much as the past. Certainly no play was worth tackling unless it offered us as the makers, the actors—and hopefully our audience—a sense of discovery, of recognition, of a new insight into the human condition. The play should *feel* as fresh as if the ink were still wet on the page.

My first season was a mixed bag with successes and duds. (In those days BBC controllers mercifully still paid lip service to the public service dictum of the "right to fail.") One of the joys of producing *Play of the Month* was the freedom it gave to cast at the highest level. Our finest actors were naturally often booked on long-running stage engagements but were usually free to rehearse during the daytime. We were still only in the afternoon of the "golden age," and I was privileged to work with many of our finest talents—Michael Gambon, John Gielgud, Kenneth Branagh, Peggy Ashcroft, Maggie Smith, Anthony Quayle, Juliet Stevenson, Anthony Hopkins, Judi Dench, Ben Kingsley, Jeremy Irons, and many more. In the next decade all the major drama strands disappeared and by the nineties single plays had dropped from over fifty to under twenty a year, on their way down to oblivion. But when in my next season I decided to approach Miller for his agreement to let us do *The Crucible,* the future for televised drama was still looking bright.

The play had been televised once before, in 1959 by Granda Television, but in a drastically cut-down version lasting only seventy-eight minutes. Miller himself described it as "scenes from the play" and was naturally chary about repeating the experience.[5] The director, Don Taylor, and I were quite clear that we wanted to do the full play as Miller wrote it, including the much-debated act 2, scene 3, where Abigail meets Proctor in the woods prior to the trial, which is still omitted from many published versions. I don't think we were averse to small cuts if we felt these might help maintain the pace and tension of the production. Television does not enjoy a captive audience, and it does not take much to lose the viewer's attention. And there was also the constant pressure from the schedulers to tighten running times. We set about the task of looking for any tightening of the text with a will, but we were forced to the conclusion that any cuts, even the smallest trims, only blurred rather than heightened Miller's extraordinary craftsmanship. That craftsmanship is nowhere more apparent than in the play's powerful opening, in which all the key elements of the drama are set running without a single line of traditional exposition.

On this basis I approached Miller with a request for the rights to go ahead with the production, and on his next visit to London (late 1979) we met for lunch at the Savoy where he was staying and where the century had not yet changed so far as to tolerate an open-necked shirt, and a necktie was offered, which Miller graciously donned. The main purpose of the lunch was for him to meet director Don Taylor, and this went well. As a result we were granted the rights, but for the United Kingdom only, which was disappointing but which the BBC accepted, and so we were set to go ahead with the production.

Don at that time was uniquely talented, intensely committed, and independently minded; he had joined the BBC directly after Oxford and early on made himself a reputation for his work with the socialist playwright David Mercer and other radical working-class writers, to whom television in the late fifties and sixties offered a vast new audience of millions whose lives and dreams had never before been reflected on so widely available a medium. It was truly a cultural revolution in which Don played a leading role, and about which he has written vividly in his book *Days of Vision.*[6]

By the time Don and I got to work together his passions were less directly political and more about the preservation of literate drama and argument, which he saw as one of television's greatest assets, from the burgeoning threat from filmed drama with its—as he saw it—obsession with images and action and rejection of language. Many of our top directors at that time were turning their backs on TV studio drama and launching out into film, which offered far greater opportunities not only in financial terms but in reputation and career possibilities. Don was never interested in this, and in the final analysis when he realized that the battle for studio drama was lost, he turned his back on television and devoted himself to writing and poetry and teaching—as well as to radio, where the nurturing of original drama has miraculously survived in the United Kingdom. But not before turning in a small number of truly outstanding productions, of which I believe *The Crucible* is a good example.

Television studio drama as developed at the BBC in those immensely creative years is today a lost art. Film has driven it into extinction. The crucial difference between the two is that where the film camera fractures the acting performance, breaking it up into a succession of shots, the TV multicamera technique allows the performance to find its own fluidity, power, and rhythms and build naturally to its own climaxes. It is the performance that dictates rather than, as so often in film, the camera and the image. And allied to this a whole generation of technicians—many of them true artists in their own right—were trained in the key skills of lighting, sound, set design, and vision-mixing that responded totally to the requirements of the performance. As in theater, text and performance were central, but the focus and selection made possible by the technology could enhance and reinforce the impact on the screen. Given the possibility of continuous performance of large segments of text, even of whole scenes, the acting could build to moments of true dramatic intensity, which film can rarely if ever achieve. Don likened it to climbing a mountain rather than a succession of small hills, and observing the process as a producer I was always aware of the huge thrill of excitement that gripped the entire studio when these moments were achieved and all the elements came together. The energy and concentration generated meant that even in the final stages of recording new discoveries in meaning, new subtleties and insights could be achieved.

This is how we recorded *The Crucible,* as essentially a live performance. In casting it Don came up with the idea of bringing together a group of our leading character actors to play the establishment figures, the judges and lawyers—faces that would be familiar to the audience—and if possible to find an unknown face for Proctor. It is more usual to cast Proctor with a star name since his is the leading role. But doing it the other way round seemed nearer to mirroring the social structure of Salem at the time. In Michael N. Harbour we found a brilliant young Royal Shakespeare Company actor who was still a new face to the wider audience, and this certainly heightened the sense of an ordinary man confronting the power and authority of a determined establishment portrayed by Eric Porter (Danforth), Daniel Massey (Reverend Hale), Peter Vaughan (Hathorne), and Denis Quilley (Reverend Parris). Mirroring reality again, we wanted to cast Abigail as young as possible, and after scouring the drama schools Don found Sarah Berger, who was still studying at the Guildhall when she landed the part.

With the production launched, the producer's role becomes secondary. The producer essentially has no job to do *in* the making of the show. He is the only one who can stand back and observe. So here I was looking again at the play that had so deeply excited me a quarter of a century before. Was it the same play?

Time had certainly weakened the correspondence between the Salem witch hunt of the play and the McCarthy witch hunt of the fifties. Salem was Salem and related more to something fundamental in human societies when gripped by fear of unknown threats than to any other particular historic episode. The parallels still stayed in the memory, but to my mind the differences now seemed to outweigh the similarities. In the characters of Deputy-Governor Danforth, Judge Hathorne, Reverend Parris, and especially Reverend Hale, Miller presented a rich portrait of the many faces of authority in all eras trying to stave off what they perceive to be the calamitous anarchy thrown up by a disintegrating social order. They are all men not villainous in intent but with recognizable human qualities and stature, some vain and petty minded, others conscious of the human tragedy around them and the weight of responsibility that lies on them. They are also to varying degrees men of compassion but aware of the danger of weakness in the face of rebellion. As I watched the rehearsals and recordings of the trial scene and the final confrontations in the prison I found myself reminded of Joan of Arc's trial in Shaw's *St. Joan.* Joan, too, was condemned to death by men who were moved by belief in the values they had to defend and the awful responsibility that went with power, as well as by others who had baser motives of greed, self-interest, and prejudice. It has been one of the great themes of tragedy from the beginning. As early as Sophocles' *Antigone,* the character of Creon, who decrees her death for refusal to submit to an inhuman law, embodies the terrifying and ultimately insoluble dilemmas of authority in the face of rebellion by those who are driven by obedience to other laws.

There were other shifts in response to the play. Proctor's last cry of defiance when he refuses to sign his name to the recantation and chooses to face death instead, in our version appeared less as a heroic clarion call on behalf of the victims of intolerance than a recognition of his own desperate need for redemption. And of the moments that stood out in my mind the most charged and disturbing now came in the scene where he is questioned by Reverend Hale about his knowledge of the Ten Commandments. He confidently reels off nine, as if by rote, none of them echoing anything we have seen so far. Then he stalls. The last one stops him. Has he forgotten or can he not bring himself to utter it? Worse still, has the awfulness of its meaning blanked it out of his mind? But it cannot be avoided, and his wife Elizabeth prompts him: "Adultery, John." And the stage direction reads: "a secret arrow had pained his heart."[7] It is a moment of stunning dramatic writing; for the first time the two themes of the play, the wretched state of his marriage to Elizabeth and the irresistible persistence of the witch-hunters' inquisition, meet and cross. Suddenly the whole dramatic situation, the heart of the play, and its inevitable tragic outcome are illuminated in one word, adultery. The dramatic thrill and pain of the moment seemed to me to shift the center of gravity of the play and raise it to a different plane.

On one level the play is certainly about witchcraft. This is its theme— the world of sorcery and black magic and devil worship that had haunted Christian Europe and was at its most troubling to the austere narrow world of Puritanism that governed the minds of the seventeenth-century settlers in New England. The additional mix of West Indian obeah, which the black slave Tituba has fed into the girls' minds, adds potency to the threat from unseen forces, which rapidly unsettles the whole province. But this does not provide the motivating force of the play. That has to be a human action and, as in many of the greatest tragedies, an action that has happened before the play starts. The precipitating action here is the very human and unmysterious adultery of Proctor with Abigail, which in the Puritan mind (and in Proctor's mind, too) was tantamount to a breach of one of the greatest taboos—lechery. This sin lurks behind all the action of the play, since it is the lust that binds them together that has let loose, through Abigail, the irrational power of witchcraft and that explodes at the end of act 3 when Proctor finally admits to the court his adultery with Abigail. It is this guilt that haunts and almost destroys Proctor and is only redeemed in the final moments of the play when he tears up his written confession; it is only then that he is able to embrace his wife and kiss her with a true and loving passion before going with some newfound sense of serenity to his death. It is the power of that redemptive moment that charges the play with its real emotional power and provided, for me at least, a very real sense of catharsis in its Aristotelian sense of purification.

In our production, thanks largely to the powerfully convincing performance of Harbour as a man of fundamental integrity and strength, the central core of the tragedy came through sharply. He is blunt and honest in his view on the hypocrisy of Reverend Parris. He has no interest in position or prestige. He abhors cant and false piety. He is a hardworking farmer who only wants to feed and support his family. He truly loves his wife. But he has allowed himself to sin in a way that releases a poison into the already corrupted world of Salem, with devastating results. In every sense Proctor is the protagonist of the play and in the classically tragic denouement he brings about his own destruction.

In this interpretation it also made no sense to drop the scene with Abigail that precedes the trial. Proctor's inner conflict has become unbearable following the arrest of Elizabeth for witchcraft. Proctor knows it is a lie and that Abigail arranged for the poppet to be planted in his house by Mary Warren in order to frame her. His own sin has now led to his wife's likely death. He is in an agony of doubt and remorse, yet Abigail still has the power to unnerve him. It is a short scene, but without it the balance of the play is too much toward the theme of witchcraft and away from the centrality of Proctor's—and Abigail's—evil knot.

In those days the BBC's program journal, *Radio Times,* published feature articles by serious writers about the coming week's shows. With this in mind I wrote to Miller to ask if he would like to consider a piece to go out in our transmission and he very kindly, in his own words, rattled something off. He titled it "Terror and the Crucible":

> Terror—being terrified—is like pain in that it is impossible to actually reproduce in the mind after it has passed. And of course extremely difficult to convey to those who have never known

it (and sometimes even to those who have). The mind tends to heal wounds, wants no more of them.

When a society has real problems and not very apt solutions for them there is a tendency for leaders to adopt [the] apocalyptic rhetoric [that] "either this is done or it is the end." And apocalypse frightens people because, after all, it just *might* be waiting *this* time. All of which tends, of course, to lodge more and more prestige and power in those who see, or pretend to see, furthest and into the darker places. Quite naturally, there is no want of people who would so pretend.[8]

In his interview with Enoch Brater in October 2000, I was fascinated by Miller's answer to a question asking him to suggest essential reading for an aspiring writer, and very high on the list came the Greeks who, he said, had played a great part in his own early dramatic education.[9] This hit me with great force, especially so since the next time Don Taylor and I worked together after *The Crucible* was on a production of *Antigone* in a modern version that Don himself wrote in collaboration with a classical Greek scholar. There was no conscious progression on our part from Miller to Sophocles, but our *Antigone* so impressed the program controller that it led us to tackle the rest of the trilogy of Theban plays of Sophocles, *Oedipus the King* and *Oedipus at Colonus*.

As I became involved in these new productions, there were still reverberating in my own mind echoes of earlier plays. I found the parallels between *The Crucible* and *Oedipus the King* fascinating. Both open with a picture of a society that is in turmoil. The people are in despair and fear some supernatural power is to blame. So the investigation begins, with ultimately devastating results.

But to return to 1980. I have called this essay "three encounters," and the third took place some months after *The Crucible* had gone out to its BBC 2 audience.

Miller had not seen our production and it seemed a good idea—especially in view of the limited distribution rights granted us—to invite him to a private screening at the BBC offices, which in those days were situated in the Rockefeller Building in New York. He accepted the invitation and brought Inge Morath, his wife, with him. I tried to put myself in a sufficiently relaxed frame of mind to get through the unnerving two-and-a-half hours ahead, but without success.

Happily there were no technical hiccups, as almost inevitably wreck such occasions. The machinery behaved. I was sufficiently distanced from the production to be able to look at it dispassionately, but my attention was constantly drawn to Miller, who sat silently throughout. Even during a brief pause to change tapes, not a word. Was he bored? Was he dismayed by what he was seeing and decided to opt for silence? Would he have any comment to make? I had a premonition of disaster.

At the end of act 3, the trial scene, a high point in the drama when Proctor has confessed to lechery and Mary Warren has failed to feign possession by spirits, the court is plunged into hysteria by the girls, led by Abigail, screaming that the devil is about to descend, and the whole room erupts into religious madness, there was another break. Again silence. After a pause Miller turned to me, smiling. "You know, Louis," he said, "it's a great . . ." I knew the word I wanted to hear, but what he actually said was, "It's a great . . . *play.*"

NOTES

1. See Arthur Miller, *Timebends: A Life* (New York: Grove Press, 1987), 417.

2. See Irving Wardle, *The Theatres of George Devine* (London: Eyre Methuen, 1978), 178.; and Gresdna A. Doty and Billy J. Harbin, eds., *Inside the Royal Court Theatre, 1956–1981: Artists Talk* (Baton Rouge: Louisiana State University Press, 1990), 32–33.

3. Arthur Miller, *The Crucible,* in *Arthur Miller's Collected Plays,* vol. 1 (New York: Viking, 1981).

4. See Victor S. Navasky, *Naming Names* (New York: Viking, 1980).

5. Arthur Miller in a personal communication to the author in 1980.

6. See Don Taylor, *Days of Vision* (London: Methuen, 1990).

7. See Miller, *The Crucible,* in *Arthur Miller's Collected Plays.*

8. See Arthur Miller, "Terror and the Crucible," *Radio Times,* July 9, 1980.

9. See Enoch Brater, ed., *Arthur Miller's America: Theater and Culture in a Time of Change* (Ann Arbor: University of Michigan Press), 244–55.

Contributors

ENOCH BRATER is the Kenneth T. Rowe Collegiate Professor of Dramatic Literature at the University of Michigan and has previously published *Arthur Miller's America: Theater and Culture in a Time of Change* and *Arthur Miller: A Playwright's Life and Works*. He is well known internationally for his seminal studies of Samuel Beckett and other leading figures in the modern and contemporary theater.

LINDA BEN-ZVI is the author of *Theater in Israel* and Professor of Theater Studies at Tel Aviv University. She has written the major biography of the American playwright Susan Glaspell and is a celebrated critic for her important writings on Samuel Beckett, Eugene O'Neill, Suzan Lori-Parks, and other major dramatists.

BELINDA KONG is Assistant Professor of Asian Studies and English at Bowdoin College. Her research and teaching focus on fiction of the Asian diaspora.

MARIAGABRIELLA CAMBIAGHI is a teacher of contemporary theater history at the Università degli Studi di Milano. She has published many studies relating to the history of drama and theatrical performance in Italy.

ROBERT GORDON is Professor of Drama at Goldsmiths College, University of London; his most recent publications include *The Purpose of Playing: Acting Theory in Perspective* and *Stoppard: Text and Performance*. He has worked as both a playwright and a director in Italy and the United Kingdom.

MICHAEL RAAB has served as dramaturg for the Staatstheater Stuttgart, the Staatstheater Mainz, the Munich Kammerspiele, and the Schauspeil Leipzig. He has written books on Shakespearean productions in Germany and England, the portrayal of the entertainment industry in contemporary British drama, the director Wolfgang Engel, and English plays in the 1990s.

DARRYL V. JONES has directed plays off-Broadway and for resident and regional companies throughout the United States, including the Arena Stage in Washington, DC, and the Old Globe in San Diego. He has been a member of the theater teaching faculty at Boston University and the University of Michigan, and currently teaches at California State University, East Bay.

MATTHEW MARTIN is a Senior Lecturer in English at St. Mary's University College, Belfast. He is the founder of the St. Mary's Writing Centre, and his research interests include contemporary Irish, English, and American drama.

JOHN T. DORSEY is Professor of English and American Literature at Rikkyo University, Tokyo. He has published numerous studies on contemporary American, Japanese, and European drama and fiction.

ANTONIO R. CELADA is a Professor in the Department of English and American Studies at the University of Salamanca, Spain. He specializes in twentieth-century English literature and American theater. He completed his doctoral dissertation on Arthur Miller and is the author of many studies of the playwright's work.

LAURA CERRATO, poet and essayist, teaches English literature at the University of Buenos Aires, where she also edits two literary reviews. She has published *Ensayos sobre poesía comparada, Doce vueltas a la literatura, Génesis de la poética Samuel Beckett,* as well as six volumes of her own poetry.

KIRSTEN HEROLD teaches in the English Department at the University of Michigan, where she concentrates on dramatic writing by Arthur Miller, Henrik Ibsen, and other socially engaged authors.

LOUIS MARKS is well known in the United Kingdom for the central role he has played as a producer for BBC television drama, where he has ranged widely in the repertory to include works by Henrik Ibsen, August Strindberg, Harold Pinter, and Arthur Miller. His highly praised adaptation of George Eliot's *Middlemarch* has been broadcast throughout the English-speaking world and beyond.